List of Contents

Introduction 1

Chapter 1: Introduction to the Pareto Law of Success 6

    1.1 What Is the Pareto Law? 6

    1.2 The Power of Small Efforts 9

    1.3 Applying the Pareto to Success 13

Chapter 2: Understanding the Pareto Principle in Depth 18

    2.1 Mathematical Foundation 18

    2.2 Real-World Examples 21

    2.3 Common Misconceptions 26

Chapter 3: Mastering the Mindset 31

    3.1 The Growth Mindset 31

    3.2 Overcoming Limiting Beliefs 35

    3.3 Visualization and Goal Setting 39

Chapter 4: Applying Pareto in Time Management 44

    4.1 Time as a Limited Resource 44

    4.2 The Pareto Productivity System 47

    4.3 Achieving Work-Life Balance 53

Chapter 5: Prioritizing Your Efforts for Maximum Impact 57

    5.1 The Art of Prioritization 57

    5.2 Pareto in Project Management 61

    5.3 Personal Prioritization Techniques 66

Chapter 6: Pareto in Business and Career Advancement 73

6.1 Pareto in Business Strategy.................................73

6.2 Career Advancement and Pareto.......................77

6.3 Entrepreneurship and Pareto 83

Chapter 7: Achieving Financial Success with Pareto.................89

7.1 Pareto and Personal Finance 89

7.2 Financial Independence and Pareto 95

7.3 Philanthropy and Pareto................................100

Chapter 8: Using Pareto to Enhance Relationships 105

8.1 Pareto in Personal Relationships 105

8.2 Networking and Pareto..................................110

8.3 Family and Pareto 114

Chapter 9: Health and Fitness: Pareto-Style.............................119

9.1 Pareto in Fitness...119

9.2 Mental Health and Well-being.......................123

9.3 Sleep and Recovery.......................................129

Chapter 10: Creativity and Pareto: Doing More with Less 136

10.1 Creative Efficiency.......................................136

10.2 Innovation and Pareto 141

10.3 Artistic Expression with Pareto 145

Chapter 11: Pareto in Education and Learning 151

11.1 Learning Effectively.....................................151

11.2 Teaching and Education...............................155

11.3 Specialized Knowledge and Expertise...........161

Chapter 12: Problem-Solving and Decision Making with Pareto
....167

12.1 Pareto-Driven Problem Solving.................................167

12.2 Decision Making for Success.............................172

12.3 Ethical Considerations.................................176

Chapter 13: Finding Balance: Pareto for a Fulfilling Life..........181

13.1 Personal Growth with Pareto 181

13.2 Balancing Multiple Life Goals.........................186

13.3 Pursuing Passion Projects 190

Chapter 14: Managing Stress and Burnout with Pareto..........196

14.1 Stress Reduction Strategies 196

14.2 Burnout Prevention and Recovery..............................200

14.3 Building Resilience 206

Chapter 15: The Pareto Lifestyle Transformation...................211

15.1 Embracing a New Way of Living...............................211

15.2 The Art of Simplicity.......................................215

15.3 Mindful Consumption 219

Conclusion..224

Introduction: The Unseen Power of Pareto

In the long journey of life, we often find ourselves entangled in the threads of effort, striving tirelessly to unravel the mysteries of success. Yet, what if I told you that there exists a hidden force—a force so potent, it can transform your life with the simplest of actions? What if I unveiled a key that could unlock the doors to unimaginable success, all while requiring the smallest of efforts?

Welcome to a journey of discovery, where we unravel the enigmatic power of the Pareto principle, a phenomenon that has quietly shaped the destinies of countless individuals, organizations, and even societies. This is not just another self-help book; this is your guide to understanding and harnessing the Pareto principle to achieve remarkable success with minimal effort.

Picture this: a handful of seeds planted in fertile soil, and from them, a lush, bountiful garden blooms. The Pareto principle, often referred to as the 80/20 rule, is like that fertile soil, where a mere fraction of your efforts can yield a bounteous harvest of rewards. It is a concept that transcends time and space, a universal truth that governs the distribution of outcomes in various facets of life.

The Pareto Principle Unveiled

Before we dive deeper into the nuances of this principle, let's unveil the essence of the Pareto principle itself.

At its core, the Pareto principle posits that roughly 80% of your outcomes result from 20% of your efforts. In other words, a small fraction of what you do—often the most strategic, efficient, or impactful actions—typically accounts for the lion's share of your achievements. The remaining 80% of your efforts, while not inconsequential, yield comparatively smaller results.

Think about it. In your life, in your work, in your pursuits, can you identify instances where a small, focused effort produced outsized results? Chances are, you've experienced the magic of Pareto at some point without even realizing it.

For instance, consider your workday. Have you noticed that a fraction of your tasks—the vital few—contribute significantly more to your overall productivity and success than the multitude of trivial tasks that seem to endlessly pile up? This is Pareto in action. It's about working smarter, not harder.

Pareto doesn't just apply to work; it permeates every facet of existence. Look at your relationships. Have you observed that a handful of people—the 20%—contribute immensely to your happiness, while the majority may have a lesser impact? Again, Pareto.

In your finances, you might find that a few investments or income streams generate most of your wealth. In your personal development, a select few habits or practices could account for most of your growth and fulfillment. And yes, even in your garden, a few choice plants may yield the majority of your harvest.

The Unseen Puppeteer

Now, you might be wondering why the Pareto principle matters. After all, it's just a mathematical observation, right? Well, that's where you'd be mistaken. Pareto isn't just a mathematical quirk; it's a life philosophy, a guiding principle, and a powerful lens through which to view the world.

Imagine, for a moment, that you possess a unique pair of glasses. When you put them on, you see the world not as it appears to the naked eye, but as it truly is—a place where the vital few exert an extraordinary influence on the trivial many. With these glasses, you can spot opportunities, prioritize tasks, and make decisions with newfound clarity and precision.

The Pareto principle, when fully embraced, transforms you into the master of your own destiny, the architect of your own success. It allows you to channel your energies where they matter most, freeing you from the shackles of unnecessary toil and enabling you to attain extraordinary results with seemingly minimal effort.

Now, here's where it gets truly fascinating. The Pareto principle is not confined to your personal sphere alone. It weaves its magic across the entire fabric of existence. Think about entire industries, nations, and civilizations. They too are subject to the rule of the vital few.

In economics, you'll find that a select handful of industries often generate the majority of a nation's wealth. In society, a small percentage of individuals might drive significant cultural or political change. In the world of ideas, a few groundbreaking theories can shape the course of scientific discovery.

This hidden force—the Pareto principle—is like an unseen puppeteer, silently pulling the strings of our lives and our world. It is the reason why a few keystrokes on a computer can launch a billion-dollar startup, why a few choice words can inspire millions, and why a few moments of profound reflection can alter the trajectory of a lifetime.

The Pareto Path to Success

Now that you've caught a glimpse of the immense power hidden within the Pareto principle, you may be wondering how to harness it for your own benefit. That, my friend, is precisely what this book is all about.

In the chapters that follow, we will embark on a journey of exploration and application. We will dive deep into the various aspects of life where Pareto's wisdom can be your guiding star. We will uncover the strategies, mindsets, and practical steps to achieve success with elegance, efficiency, and grace.

You'll learn how to prioritize your efforts, streamline your work, nurture fruitful relationships, attain financial abundance, and find balance in the hustle and bustle of modern life—all while exerting the smallest of efforts. This is not about shortcuts or quick fixes; it's about working in harmony with the natural laws that govern our world.

So, dear reader, prepare to be enlightened, empowered, and transformed. As we venture deeper into the realms of

Pareto's magic, remember this: within the 20% lies the key to 80% of your success. Your journey toward becoming a Pareto master begins now.

Chapter 1: Introduction to the Pareto Law of Success

1.1 What Is the Pareto Law?

Imagine a world where you could achieve more with less effort, where your actions, decisions, and investments yield results beyond your wildest dreams. It's not an elusive fantasy but a reality waiting to be discovered through the Pareto Law of Success, a powerful principle that has transformed the lives of countless individuals.

The 80/20 Rule Explained

At the heart of the Pareto Law of Success lies a simple yet profound concept - the 80/20 rule. Named after the Italian economist Vilfredo Pareto, this principle asserts that roughly 80% of effects come from 20% of causes. In practical terms, it means that a small portion of your efforts often leads to the majority of your results.

Imagine you're a salesperson, and you notice that 20% of your clients contribute to 80% of your revenue. This isn't an anomaly but a consistent pattern observed across various domains. In your work, you might find that 20% of your tasks generate 80% of your productivity. In your personal life, you may discover that 20% of your relationships bring you 80% of your happiness and fulfillment.

Understanding the 80/20 rule is like wielding a magic wand for efficiency. It allows you to pinpoint the vital few factors that drive your success, directing your focus and resources where they matter most. By doing so, you can achieve exceptional results while conserving time and energy.

Historical Background

Before we delve deeper into the practical applications of the Pareto Law of Success, let's take a brief journey back in time to understand its historical roots.

Vilfredo Pareto, an Italian economist and philosopher, introduced this principle in the early 20th century. He initially observed it while studying wealth distribution in his home country, where he noticed that approximately 20% of the population owned around 80% of the land. Intrigued by this imbalance, Pareto delved further, applying the principle to other aspects of life.

His groundbreaking insight soon found applications in diverse fields, ranging from economics and business to sociology and personal development. Today, the Pareto principle stands as a timeless testament to the uneven distribution of effects, transcending boundaries and cultures.

Applicability in Various Aspects of Life

The beauty of the Pareto Law of Success lies in its versatility. It's not confined to a single domain; rather, it permeates virtually every aspect of life. Let's explore how this principle can be applied in various areas to unlock your true potential.

1. Business and Career: In the world of business, the Pareto principle often manifests as the 20% of customers who generate 80% of profits, or the 20% of employees who contribute to 80% of a company's success. Identifying these key players allows businesses to optimize their strategies and resources.

2. Time Management: In your daily life, you'll find that 20% of your tasks are responsible for 80% of your productivity. By focusing on these high-impact activities, you can supercharge your time management skills, leaving more room for personal growth and leisure.

3. Relationships: The Pareto principle applies to your social life as well. Typically, 20% of your relationships provide 80% of your emotional support and joy. Recognizing and nurturing these connections fosters deeper, more meaningful bonds.

4. Personal Development: When it comes to self-improvement, not all efforts are created equal. 20% of your habits and routines often lead to 80% of your personal growth. By identifying and reinforcing these habits, you can accelerate your journey toward becoming the best version of yourself.

5. Financial Management: In personal finance, the Pareto principle can help you allocate your resources wisely. Often, 20% of your financial decisions lead to 80% of your wealth accumulation. By making strategic choices, you can secure your financial future.

The Pareto principle serves as a powerful lens through which you can view the world. It empowers you to distinguish between the trivial many and the vital few, guiding your actions toward maximum impact. It's not a mere theory but a tool for practical transformation, and in the chapters ahead, we will explore how to apply it to every facet of your life.

Keep in mind that the Pareto Law of Success is not a quick fix or a shortcut to success. Instead, it's a philosophy that encourages you to work smarter, not harder. It's about making conscious choices, embracing efficiency, and achieving more with less. So, let's dive deeper into the intricacies of this transformative principle and uncover the secrets to winning big with the smallest efforts.

1.2 The Power of Small Efforts

In this journey towards understanding the Pareto Law of Success, we embark on a profound exploration of how small efforts can yield remarkable results. We're about to uncover a secret that has the potential to transform your life in ways you never imagined. It's a secret that goes against the grain of conventional wisdom, a secret that challenges the myth of hard work, and a secret that sets the stage for your ultimate success.

The Myth of Hard Work

From a young age, we are instilled with the belief that success comes from working tirelessly, burning the midnight oil, and sacrificing our leisure time for the pursuit of our goals. The message is clear: if you want to make it big, you must put in immense effort and sweat. While hard work undoubtedly plays a role in achieving success, the Pareto Law suggests that it's not the quantity of effort but the quality that truly matters.

Picture this: you're in a vast forest with a machete in your hand. You can choose to hack away at every tree in your path, expending tremendous energy, but you'll make slow progress. Alternatively, you can use that same energy to identify the tallest, most significant trees and focus your efforts on them. By doing so, you clear a path much more efficiently and with far less exhaustion.

This is the essence of the Pareto principle - the realization that 20% of your efforts often lead to 80% of your results. It's about working smarter, not harder. When you shift your perspective from the quantity of work to the quality of your efforts, you open the door to a world where success becomes attainable with less strain and greater effectiveness.

Leveraging the 20% for Maximum Impact

Now that we've dispelled the myth of hard work, let's delve deeper into the concept of leveraging the vital 20% for maximum impact. This is where the magic truly happens.

Imagine you're managing a project with ten tasks on your to-do list. Historically, you might have tackled each task with equal zeal and commitment, spreading your time and energy evenly. However, the Pareto principle encourages you to pause and reassess.

Upon closer examination, you discover that two of these tasks are significantly more critical than the others. These two tasks have the potential to propel your project forward with minimal effort compared to the remaining eight. By concentrating your energy and resources on these pivotal tasks, you can expedite your progress and achieve your goals faster.

This isn't about cutting corners or neglecting important responsibilities. It's about recognizing that not all tasks carry equal weight in determining your success. By identifying and prioritizing the tasks that yield the most substantial results, you can work efficiently, leaving you with more time and energy to allocate elsewhere.

The concept of leverage extends beyond mere task management. It applies to every facet of your life, from personal development to career advancement. By pinpointing the critical 20% and directing your efforts there, you maximize your impact and open doors to opportunities that might have otherwise remained hidden.

Setting the Stage for Success
Now that we understand the power of small efforts and the significance of focusing on the vital few, it's time to set the

stage for your success. The Pareto principle is not a one-size-fits-all solution; it's a framework that can be tailored to your unique goals and aspirations.

Begin by defining what success means to you. Is it achieving financial independence, excelling in your career, nurturing fulfilling relationships, or finding personal happiness? Success takes many forms, and it's crucial to clarify your vision. Once you've set your objectives, you can apply the Pareto principle strategically.

Let's take an example: suppose your goal is to become a proficient guitarist. Instead of spending hours practicing various techniques haphazardly, identify the essential skills that will have the most significant impact on your progress. It could be mastering chord transitions, fingerpicking, or scales. Dedicate the majority of your practice time to these critical elements, and you'll notice substantial improvement in a shorter period.

Furthermore, remember that success is a journey, not a destination. The Pareto principle isn't a quick-fix solution; it's a mindset shift that allows you to approach your goals with greater clarity and efficiency. Embrace the idea that achieving success often requires patience and persistence.

In this chapter, we've merely scratched the surface of the Pareto Law of Success. As we journey through the following chapters, you'll discover how this principle applies to various aspects of your life, from time management to personal development, and how it can revolutionize your approach to success. It's time to embark on this transformative journey, where small efforts yield monumental results. Get ready to witness the power of the Pareto principle in action and change the trajectory of your life forever.

1.3 Applying the Pareto to Success

In this exhilarating journey toward success, we'll embark on a transformational voyage, one where you'll discover the incredible power of the Pareto Principle—the 80/20 rule—applied to your life. After the end of this book, you'll be equipped with a fresh perspective, ready to unleash your potential, transform your mindset, and achieve more with less effort than you ever thought possible.

Unleashing Your Potential

Have you ever felt like there's an untapped reservoir of potential within you, waiting to be unleashed? Well, my friend, you're not alone. We all possess an abundance of untapped potential, often hidden beneath layers of self-doubt, fear, and the misconception that success requires Herculean effort. But here's the secret: your potential is like a dormant volcano, and the Pareto Principle is the catalyst that will awaken it.

Imagine your potential as a wellspring of creativity, innovation, and achievement. By applying the Pareto Principle, you can channel your efforts toward the 20% that generates 80% of your results. It's like having a treasure map that guides you to the most valuable opportunities in your life.

So, how do you begin to unleash this dormant potential? It starts with a shift in perspective. Instead of feeling overwhelmed by the sheer magnitude of your goals, focus on the vital few tasks that truly matter. Identify the 20% of activities that will yield 80% of your desired outcomes.

For example, if you're an aspiring writer, instead of spending hours writing aimlessly, concentrate on the core 20%—the most impactful words, ideas, and stories that will captivate your readers. This targeted approach not only conserves your energy but also maximizes your creativity and productivity.

Think of your potential as a powerful river. It flows most vigorously when it's confined to a narrow channel. Similarly, your potential surges when you channel your efforts into the vital few tasks that align with your goals and values.

Now, let's dive even deeper. Unleashing your potential also involves self-belief and self-mastery. The Pareto Principle isn't just about efficiency; it's about becoming the best version of yourself. As you journey toward success, cultivate a growth mindset. Embrace challenges as opportunities for growth, and learn from failures as stepping stones to achievement.

Remember, successful individuals like Thomas Edison and Elon Musk didn't achieve greatness by shying away from challenges. They embraced setbacks as valuable lessons, which ultimately propelled them to unparalleled success. So, dare to dream big, push your limits, and, most importantly, believe in your ability to turn your potential into reality.

Transforming Your Mindset

Now, let's delve into the transformative power of your mindset. Your mind is a remarkable instrument, capable of shaping your reality. However, it can also be your greatest obstacle if not harnessed correctly. The Pareto Principle guides us toward a mindset shift that can make all the difference in your journey to success.

Imagine your mindset as a lens through which you view the world. If that lens is clouded with negativity, self-doubt, and limiting beliefs, it distorts your perception of opportunities and hinders your ability to seize them. Conversely, a clear and empowered mindset acts as a powerful filter, allowing you to see the potential for success even in challenging situations.

So, how can you transform your mindset using the Pareto Principle? Start by challenging your limiting beliefs. Recognize that you don't need to do it all or work tirelessly around the clock to achieve success. Instead, focus on the 20% of efforts that will yield the majority of your results.

Moreover, embrace a growth mindset, which thrives on challenges and sees failures as stepping stones. Cultivate resilience in the face of setbacks, and maintain a positive attitude toward learning and growth. Your mindset is not a fixed entity; it's a flexible, adaptable tool that can be honed to serve your goals.

Achieving More with Less

Now, here's where the magic truly happens: achieving more with less. It's a concept that might sound counterintuitive in a world that often glorifies overwork and busyness. However, when you harness the Pareto Principle, you'll discover the incredible efficiency of focused effort.

Think about your to-do list. How many tasks are on there that, if you're honest with yourself, won't significantly move the needle toward your goals? It's a common trap to fall into—the idea that the more you do, the more successful you'll become. But here's the reality: success isn't about doing everything; it's about doing the right things.

The Pareto Principle encourages you to identify the critical few tasks that will propel you forward. It's about prioritization, not procrastination. By concentrating your efforts on the most impactful activities, you'll find that you accomplish more with less time and energy.

Imagine you're an entrepreneur launching a new product. Rather than spreading yourself thin across a multitude of marketing channels, focus on the 20% that brings in 80% of your customers. This targeted approach not only saves time but also increases the effectiveness of your marketing efforts.

In your personal life, too, the Pareto Principle can work wonders. Consider the time you spend on hobbies, relationships, and self-improvement. By honing in on the 20% of activities that provide 80% of your satisfaction and growth, you'll find more time for what truly matters to you.

In essence, the Pareto Principle is your ally in simplifying complexity, streamlining your efforts, and achieving remarkable results with efficiency. It's about working smarter, not harder, and realizing that less can truly be more when guided by intention and purpose.

As we journey deeper into the Pareto Principle, you'll discover how to apply these concepts to various aspects of your life, from time management and productivity to personal development and relationships. The road to success is paved with intention, and the Pareto Principle will be your trusty guide along the way.

So, my fellow explorer of success, take these insights to heart. Unleash your potential, transform your mindset, and start achieving more with less. Your journey toward a life of purpose, productivity, and fulfillment has only just begun. The best is yet to come.

Chapter 2: Understanding the Pareto Principle in Depth

2.1 Mathematical Foundation

Welcome to the intriguing world of the Pareto Principle, where we'll embark on a journey to unveil the mathematical foundation that underpins this powerful concept. Fear not, for this exploration is an exciting and enlightening one, and it holds the potential to transform the way you approach your goals and aspirations.

The Pareto Distribution

Let's begin with a fundamental question: What is the Pareto Distribution, and why does it matter to you? Imagine this scenario: you're sitting at your kitchen table, sifting through your monthly expenses, and you notice something peculiar. A small fraction of your expenditures, roughly 20%, is responsible for a staggering 80% of your total costs. This observation forms the essence of the Pareto Principle, and it finds its roots in the Pareto Distribution.

Vilfredo Pareto, an Italian economist, was the first to notice this phenomenon in the early 20th century when he realized that approximately 20% of the population in Italy owned a whopping 80% of the land. His curiosity piqued, Pareto began exploring other domains and found that this principle held true in various contexts, from wealth distribution to productivity and beyond.

Now, you may be wondering, "How does this relate to my life?" The answer lies in the profound implications of the

Pareto Distribution. It serves as a reminder that not all efforts, actions, or resources are created equal. In fact, a small portion often generates the lion's share of results. Understanding this concept empowers you to work smarter, not harder.

Identifying the Critical 20%

So, what's the key takeaway here? The Pareto Principle encourages you to identify that crucial 20%. In your daily life, this might mean recognizing the 20% of tasks or activities that contribute to 80% of your outcomes. It's about honing in on the vital actions that bring you the most value.

Consider your work responsibilities, for instance. More often than not, a small subset of your tasks significantly influences your success. By pinpointing this critical 20%, you can prioritize your efforts and direct your energy where it will make the most substantial impact.

But it's not limited to the workplace. Apply this principle to your personal life as well. Focus on the 20% of activities that bring you the most joy, fulfillment, or personal growth. By doing so, you can create more time and space for the things that genuinely matter to you.

Implications for Goal Setting

Now, let's dive into an area where the Pareto Principle truly shines: goal setting. When you set goals, you can leverage this principle to your advantage by identifying the 20% of actions that will lead to 80% of your desired results.

Picture yourself aiming for a promotion at work. Instead of spreading yourself thin across a multitude of tasks, your path to success becomes clearer. By zeroing in on the key actions that promise the most significant impact on your career advancement—whether it involves acquiring specific skills, strategically networking, or taking on high-impact projects—you increase your chances of success while making the journey more manageable.

The beauty of the Pareto Principle lies not only in its efficiency but also in its effectiveness. It challenges conventional approaches and urges you to seek strategies that yield substantial results with minimal effort. It's akin to finding a treasure map that guides you directly to the treasure chest, sparing you from aimless wandering.

In essence, the Pareto Principle compels you to work smarter, not harder. It invites you to question traditional methodologies and uncover approaches that optimize both your time and efforts. The result? Enhanced productivity, reduced stress, and a more streamlined path toward your aspirations.

The Pareto Principle, rooted in the Pareto Distribution, equips you with the tools to identify the vital 20% in any aspect of your life. It serves as a potent tool for efficient and effective goal setting. By comprehending and applying this principle, you'll not only achieve more with less effort but also discover a greater sense of fulfillment and balance in your pursuit of success. As you embark on this journey of exploration, keep an open mind, and prepare to revolutionize the way you approach your goals and dreams.

2.2 Real-World Examples

Welcome to the heart of the Pareto Principle, where we delve deep into the real-world applications that make this principle a game-changer in our quest for success and efficiency. In this chapter, we'll explore a treasure trove of examples that illustrate how the 80/20 rule plays out in various aspects of our lives. Prepare to be amazed, because the Pareto Principle is more than just a theory; it's a practical tool that can transform your approach to business, personal productivity, and so much more.

Business Success Stories

Let's start with the realm of business, where the Pareto Principle has left an indelible mark on some of the world's most successful companies. In fact, this principle often guides their decision-making and resource allocation.

Case Studies 1: Identifying High-Value Customers

Consider the case of Amazon, the e-commerce giant that disrupted the retail industry. Amazon's success isn't merely due to its vast inventory and speedy delivery. It's rooted in its ability to identify and cater to its high-value customers—the 20% who generate 80% of the revenue. By understanding their preferences and tailoring recommendations, Amazon maximizes its profitability while enhancing customer satisfaction. This is the power of Pareto in customer relationship management.

Case Studies 2: Streamlining Business Processes

Now, let's turn our attention to General Electric (GE), a global conglomerate known for its diverse portfolio. GE employed the Pareto Principle to optimize its operations. By identifying the 20% of products that contributed to 80% of their profits, they streamlined their production processes, reduced costs, and increased efficiency. This strategic approach allowed GE to maintain its competitive edge in various industries.

Case Studies 3: Maximizing Profit Margins

Apple, the tech giant that needs no introduction, is another shining example. Apple's relentless focus on innovation isn't just about creating cutting-edge products; it's about maximizing profit margins. By identifying and enhancing the features that matter most to their customers, Apple has maintained premium pricing while providing superior value. In doing so, they've become a prime example of how Pareto principles can drive profitability.

These business success stories aren't isolated incidents; they exemplify how the Pareto Principle can be harnessed to achieve remarkable results. By directing your efforts toward the critical 20%, you can unlock the full potential of your business endeavors.

Personal Productivity Examples
The Pareto Principle isn't limited to boardrooms and balance sheets; it's equally transformative in the realm of personal productivity. Let's explore how it can turbocharge your efficiency in everyday life.

Case Studies 1: Pareto-Driven Time Management

Imagine you're faced with a towering to-do list, and time seems to slip through your fingers like sand. This is where the Pareto Principle can step in as your guiding light. By identifying the 20% of tasks that yield 80% of your results, you can prioritize effectively. Focus your energy on these high-impact tasks, and watch your productivity soar.

Let's say you're a writer, working on a book (much like this one). Instead of spending equal time on every chapter, you can identify the chapters that resonate most with your readers, and concentrate your efforts there. This targeted approach not only saves time but also ensures that your work has a more significant impact.

Case Studies 2: Pareto and Digital Detox

In an era of constant connectivity, digital distractions can derail our productivity. The Pareto Principle offers a remedy. Consider your digital interactions—social media, email, and messaging apps. You'll likely find that 20% of your online activities consume 80% of your time. By reducing or eliminating these non-essential activities, you can regain precious hours in your day.

Take a page from Tim Ferriss, author of "The 4-Hour Workweek." He advocates a digital detox known as the "low-information diet." By selectively consuming information and focusing on what truly matters, he's able to accomplish more in less time.

Case Studies 3: Pareto in Goal Setting

Setting goals is a fundamental aspect of personal development, but not all goals are created equal. The Pareto Principle teaches us to discriminate between the vital few and the trivial many. Instead of spreading yourself thin by pursuing numerous goals simultaneously, concentrate your efforts on the 20% of goals that will have the most significant impact on your life.

For instance, if you aim to improve your physical fitness, identify the exercises and dietary changes that will yield the most results. By zeroing in on these key areas, you can expedite your progress and achieve your fitness goals with less effort.

Applying the Principle Everywhere

Now that we've glimpsed the power of the Pareto Principle in business and personal productivity, let's explore how it can be applied virtually anywhere. It's a universal concept with limitless applications.

Case Studies 1: Pareto in Timeless Wisdom

Ancient wisdom often aligns with the principles of Pareto. Take Confucius, for instance, who emphasized the importance of focusing on essentials. His famous saying, "Real knowledge is to know the extent of one's ignorance," echoes the Pareto Principle's message: prioritize what truly matters.

Case Studies 2: Pareto and Environmental Sustainability

Environmentalists also recognize the value of the 80/20 rule. By identifying the 20% of environmental issues responsible for 80% of our ecological challenges, we can channel our efforts into addressing the most critical concerns, such as climate change and habitat loss. In this way, the Pareto Principle empowers us to be more effective advocates for our planet.

Case Studies 3: Pareto for Effective Parenting

Even in the realm of parenting, the Pareto Principle can offer valuable guidance. Parents can identify the 20% of actions and behaviors that lead to 80% of their children's development and happiness. By focusing on these key areas, parents can provide the most nurturing and supportive environment for their children's growth.

As we've journeyed through these real-world examples, it's clear that the Pareto Principle is more than just a theory—it's a transformative tool that empowers us to maximize our efforts and achieve exceptional results. By applying this principle strategically, whether in business, personal productivity, or other facets of life, you're setting yourself on a path to success and fulfillment that's both efficient and effective. So, seize the power of Pareto and watch your life transform before your eyes.

2.3 Common Misconceptions

In our journey to grasp the true essence of the Pareto Principle, it's essential to shed light on the common misconceptions that often cloud our understanding. These myths, if left unchallenged, can hinder our ability to harness the power of this transformative principle effectively. Let's embark on a journey of myth-busting and clarity.

Debunking Myths

Myth #1: The 80/20 Rule is Always Exact

The first myth we need to debunk is the belief that the Pareto Principle is an absolute, unchanging law. While it's often expressed as the 80/20 rule, the specific ratios can vary. In some cases, it might be 70/30, 90/10, or even 95/5. The key lies in recognizing that the principle signifies an imbalance where a minority of efforts or inputs often yield the majority of results. This adaptability makes the principle a versatile tool rather than a rigid doctrine.

Myth #2: It's Always About "Work Less, Achieve More"

Another misconception is that the Pareto Principle is synonymous with laziness or shortcuts. It's not about evading hard work; rather, it's about directing your efforts where they matter most. Imagine you're gardening, and you notice that 20% of your plants are producing 80% of the blooms. Focusing your attention on these thriving plants doesn't mean you're avoiding the labor; you're optimizing it for maximum beauty.

Myth #3: Pareto is Limited to Business

Some believe that the Pareto Principle exclusively applies to the business world. While it indeed has profound implications for businesses, its reach extends far beyond boardrooms and profit margins. It can enhance your personal life, improve relationships, and help you achieve your goals, whatever they may be. The 80/20 lens offers a fresh perspective on everyday challenges.

Myth #4: The Principle is Static

Many assume that the Pareto Principle remains static over time. In reality, the principle's dynamics can shift. What was once a "vital few" in your life or work may evolve, requiring you to reassess and adapt your strategy. Don't treat your initial insights as immutable; they're stepping stones on your journey to continued improvement.

Recognizing When It Doesn't Apply
While the Pareto Principle is a powerful tool, it's crucial to recognize situations where it might not apply as effectively:

Situation #1: In the Early Stages of a Project

In the initial phases of a project, it's challenging to distinguish the vital few from the trivial many. At this point, you might need to invest more evenly across various tasks until you gather enough data to identify the key areas deserving of your focus.

Situation #2: Complex and Interconnected Systems

In intricate systems with numerous dependencies, applying the 80/20 rule might be challenging. In such cases, consider a broader perspective, focusing on optimizing the entire system rather than isolating individual components.

Situation #3: Emotional and Human Factors

Human relationships and emotions rarely conform to neat ratios. While the Pareto Principle can provide insights into your relationships, remember that emotions, motivations, and behaviors are often multifaceted and fluid.

Avoiding Pitfalls
Pitfall #1: Neglecting the 20%

One common pitfall is to overlook the significance of the 20%. It's easy to get caught up in the less critical tasks, thinking they deserve equal attention. To avoid this, periodically assess your efforts and make sure you're investing your time and resources where they have the most impact.

Pitfall #2: Over-Applying Pareto

While the Pareto Principle is a valuable tool, it's not the only lens through which to view the world. Over-reliance on this principle can lead to oversimplification and missed opportunities. Remember that complexity exists, and sometimes it's necessary to dig deeper and explore nuances.

Pitfall #3: Inflexible Thinking

Avoid rigid thinking when applying the Pareto Principle. Adaptability is key. Be open to recalibrating your focus as circumstances change. What worked yesterday might not work tomorrow, and that's perfectly fine.

The Pareto Principle is a versatile and dynamic concept that can significantly enhance your life. By debunking myths, recognizing when it doesn't apply, and avoiding common pitfalls, you'll be better equipped to harness its power effectively. Embrace the principle as a valuable tool in your journey toward greater productivity, efficiency, and success.

Chapter 3: Mastering the Mindset

3.1 The Growth Mindset

In the journey towards success, the foundation is often built upon the strength of your mindset. One of the most powerful and transformative mindsets you can cultivate is the growth mindset. This mindset isn't just a buzzword; it's a profound shift in the way you approach challenges, handle setbacks, and ultimately, navigate the path to achieving your dreams. So, let's dive deep into the growth mindset and understand how embracing challenges, cultivating persistence, and learning from failure can propel you towards unparalleled success.

Embracing Challenges

Picture this: You're faced with a daunting task, something that seems beyond your current abilities. The fixed mindset says, "I can't do it; it's too hard," while the growth mindset counters, "I may not be able to do it yet, but I can learn and improve." This is where the magic begins.

Embracing challenges with a growth mindset means approaching them not as insurmountable obstacles but as opportunities for growth. When you encounter something difficult, rather than shying away, lean into it. This mindset shift is akin to stepping onto a path paved with possibilities.

It all starts with reframing your thoughts. Instead of dwelling on your limitations, focus on your potential. Embrace challenges as chances to stretch your abilities and expand your skillset. By doing so, you're not just facing adversity; you're actively seeking out opportunities to become better.

Imagine the most successful people you know. They didn't reach their heights by staying in their comfort zones. They embraced challenges, sought out new experiences, and used each obstacle as a stepping stone towards their goals. The growth mindset encourages you to do the same.

Cultivating Persistence

Persistence is the secret sauce that turns dreams into reality. It's the unwavering commitment to your goals, the determination to keep going when the going gets tough. In the world of the growth mindset, persistence isn't optional; it's a way of life.

When you're on a path of growth, setbacks are part of the journey. However, it's how you respond to those setbacks that makes all the difference. A growth mindset doesn't see failure as the end but as a stepping stone towards success. It views setbacks as opportunities to learn, adapt, and persevere.

Cultivating persistence means understanding that success is rarely a linear path. There will be twists, turns, and moments when you question your abilities. But in those moments, remember that it's not about how many times you fall; it's about how many times you get back up.

To cultivate persistence, set clear goals and remind yourself of your "why." When you have a strong sense of purpose, it becomes easier to stay committed, even in the face of adversity. Break your goals into manageable steps, and celebrate small victories along the way. Each step forward, no matter how small, is a testament to your persistence.

Learning from Failure

Failure is a word that often carries a negative connotation, but in the realm of the growth mindset, it's a valuable teacher. Instead of fearing failure, embrace it as a necessary part of the learning process.

Every time you try and fall short, you're given an opportunity to gather insights and improve. The growth mindset understands that success isn't about never failing; it's about failing forward. It's about taking each failure as a lesson that brings you closer to your goals.

Think of failure as a scientist might. When an experiment doesn't yield the expected results, a scientist doesn't give up on the entire project. Instead, they carefully analyze what went wrong, make adjustments, and try again. This iterative process leads to breakthroughs.

Similarly, when you face a setback or failure, take a step back and ask yourself: What can I learn from this? What adjustments can I make? How can I grow from this experience?

Consider the story of J.K. Rowling, the author of the immensely popular Harry Potter series. Before achieving fame and success, she faced numerous rejections from publishers. It was in these moments of rejection that she learned to refine her writing and storytelling skills. Her resilience and ability to learn from failure ultimately led to her becoming one of the most celebrated authors of our time.

In the growth mindset, there's no such thing as a dead-end. There are only detours, opportunities to learn, and chances to become better than you were yesterday.

As you embark on your journey of embracing challenges, cultivating persistence, and learning from failure with a growth mindset, remember that it's not about instant success. It's about the process, the progress, and the person you become along the way.

When challenges arise, see them as invitations to grow. When persistence is required, tap into your inner reservoir of determination. When failure occurs, embrace it as a stepping stone on your path to success. This is the essence of the growth mindset, a mindset that propels you toward your dreams with unwavering confidence and a spirit of resilience.

So, as you navigate the challenges and triumphs of life, carry with you the wisdom of the growth mindset, for it will not only shape your success but also transform you into the best version of yourself—one step, one challenge, and one failure at a time.

3.2 Overcoming Limiting Beliefs

In this journey of personal transformation, we arrive at a pivotal juncture — the art of overcoming limiting beliefs. This subchapter is your gateway to demolishing self-imposed barriers and forging a path toward unbridled success. Together, we will delve deep into the intricacies of identifying negative thought patterns, replacing them with empowering beliefs, and building unshakable self-confidence.

Identifying Negative Thought Patterns

To embark on a journey of self-improvement, we must first become aware of the mental roadblocks holding us back. Negative thought patterns, often deeply ingrained from our past experiences and societal conditioning, are like heavy anchors preventing us from soaring to our fullest potential.

Negative thought patterns manifest in various forms:

1. Self-Doubt: The nagging inner voice that questions your abilities and worthiness. It tells you that you're not good enough, smart enough, or talented enough to succeed.

2. Fear of Failure: This paralyzing fear keeps you from taking risks and stepping out of your comfort zone. It convinces you that failure is the end of the road rather than a stepping stone to success.

3. Perfectionism: The relentless pursuit of flawlessness, which often leads to procrastination and self-criticism. Perfectionism is the enemy of progress.

4. Catastrophizing: This involves always expecting the worst possible outcome in any situation. It magnifies problems and underestimates your ability to handle challenges.

5. Comparing Yourself to Others: Constantly measuring your worth against others' achievements can lead to feelings of inadequacy and envy.

To conquer these negative thought patterns, start by simply observing your thoughts without judgment. Take note of when these limiting beliefs arise and in what situations. Awareness is the first step in breaking free from their grip.

Replacing Limiting Beliefs
Once you've identified these thought patterns, it's time to replace them with empowering beliefs that support your growth and success. This process is akin to weeding a garden to allow vibrant flowers to thrive. Here's how to do it:

1. Challenge the Negative Belief: Question the validity of your limiting belief. Is there concrete evidence to support it? Often, you'll find that these beliefs are based on assumptions rather than facts.

2. Rewrite the Narrative: Craft a new, positive belief that counters the negative one. For example, if you've always believed you're not good at public speaking, replace it with, "I am improving my public speaking skills with each opportunity."

3. Affirmations: Use daily affirmations to reinforce your new beliefs. Repeating affirmations like, "I am confident and capable" or "I embrace challenges as opportunities for growth" can gradually reshape your mindset.

4. Visualization: Visualize yourself succeeding in areas where you previously held limiting beliefs. The mind is a powerful tool, and visualizing success can help reprogram your subconscious.

5. Seek Support: Share your journey with a trusted friend, coach, or therapist who can provide guidance and encouragement. Sometimes, an external perspective can shed light on blind spots in your thinking.

Remember, replacing limiting beliefs is an ongoing process. Be patient with yourself, and don't be discouraged by occasional setbacks. It takes time to rewire thought patterns that may have been ingrained for years.

Building Self-Confidence
As you break free from the shackles of limiting beliefs, you'll notice a remarkable transformation in your self-confidence. Confidence is the fuel that propels you forward on your path to success. It's the unwavering belief in your abilities, even in the face of adversity.

Here's how to cultivate and strengthen your self-confidence:

1. Set Small Goals: Start with achievable goals that push you just beyond your comfort zone. Each success, no matter how small, boosts your confidence.

2. Celebrate Your Wins: Acknowledge and celebrate your accomplishments, no matter how minor they may seem. These victories serve as evidence of your competence.

3. Positive Self-Talk: Replace self-criticism with self-encouragement. Speak to yourself as you would to a dear friend, with kindness and support.

4. Embrace Failure: Understand that failure is not a reflection of your worth. It's a stepping stone on the path to success. Learn from your mistakes and keep moving forward.

5. Expand Your Comfort Zone: Continually seek opportunities to challenge yourself and expand your skill set. With each new experience, your confidence grows.

6. Surround Yourself with Positivity: Surround yourself with people who uplift and support you. Avoid those who constantly undermine your self-worth.

7. Self-Care: Taking care of your physical and mental well-being is crucial for building confidence. A healthy lifestyle, including exercise, balanced nutrition, and adequate rest, contributes to a positive self-image.

Remember, self-confidence is not an all-or-nothing attribute. It's a spectrum, and everyone experiences moments of doubt. The key is to develop the resilience to bounce back from setbacks and continue moving forward.

By identifying negative thought patterns, replacing limiting beliefs with empowering ones, and nurturing self-confidence, you'll unleash a newfound sense of self that paves the way for unparalleled success. You have the power to sculpt your mindset into a force that propels you toward your goals with unwavering determination and boundless confidence.

3.3 Visualization and Goal Setting

In this subchapter, we're about to embark on a remarkable journey that has the potential to transform your life. We'll delve into the power of visualization, explore how SMART goals align seamlessly with the Pareto principle, and guide you in crafting a vision for success that's not just compelling but also actionable.

The Power of Visualization

Close your eyes for a moment and imagine a vivid mental image of your most cherished goal. Whether it's landing your dream job, achieving financial independence, or mastering a new skill, take a mental snapshot of what success looks like to you.

Visualization is a potent tool that can supercharge your journey towards success. When you immerse yourself in a detailed mental picture of your goals, something extraordinary happens within your brain. You see, your brain doesn't distinguish between the experiences you have in the physical world and those you vividly imagine. It treats both as real.

Imagine yourself as the successful entrepreneur you aspire to be. See the thriving business, feel the sense of accomplishment, hear the applause from your peers – these mental experiences are powerful motivators. They wire your brain for success, creating neural pathways that make achieving your goals more likely.

SMART Goals and Pareto

Now, let's marry the concept of visualization with a goal-setting framework that harmonizes seamlessly with the Pareto principle: SMART goals. This acronym stands for Specific, Measurable, Achievable, Relevant, and Time-bound. Let's break down each component:

1. Specific: Your goals should be crystal clear. Instead of setting a vague goal like "I want to be successful," define it more precisely, such as "I want to become a renowned author."

2. Measurable: A goal should be quantifiable. How will you measure your progress? Perhaps you'll measure success by the number of books published, positive reader reviews, or revenue generated.

3. Achievable: While it's crucial to dream big, your goals should be within reach. An achievable goal ensures you don't set yourself up for frustration. If you've never written before, aiming to write a bestselling novel next month might not be realistic.

4. Relevant: Your goal should align with your values and long-term objectives. Does becoming a renowned author resonate with your passions and values? If not, it might not be the right goal for you.

5. Time-bound: Without a deadline, a goal can languish indefinitely. Set a specific timeframe for achieving your goal, which adds a sense of urgency and keeps you accountable.

Here's where the beauty of Pareto enters the scene. When you apply the Pareto principle to SMART goals, you'll find that a significant portion of your results often comes from a focused effort on just a few aspects of your goal. Identify the vital 20% of your goal that will yield 80% of your desired outcomes. This Pareto-inspired approach enhances the precision of your goals and increases your likelihood of success.

For instance, if your goal is to social media success, the critical 20% might involve outlining your plans structure, setting a posting schedule, and actively seeking your follower feedback. These actions, when pursued with determination, will drive the majority of your account success.

Crafting Your Vision for Success
Now, it's time to craft a compelling vision for your success. This isn't merely about setting goals; it's about painting a vivid picture of what your life will look like when you've

achieved those goals. Think of your vision as the North Star guiding your journey.

Start by asking yourself some profound questions:

- What does success mean to you?

- How will your life be different when you've achieved your goals?

- How do you envision your daily routine in this successful future?

- What impact will your success have on the people around you?

Imagine the smallest details. Picture the joy on your face as you hold your published book for the first time, smell the fresh pages, feel the texture of the cover, and hear the sound of pages turning as readers immerse themselves in your words.

As you craft this vision, let your emotions run free. Connect with the deep-seated feelings of accomplishment, joy, and fulfillment that success will bring. Emotions are the fuel that propels you forward.

To solidify your vision, consider creating a vision board. Collect images, quotes, and symbols that represent your goals and arrange them on a board. Place it where you'll see it daily, and let it serve as a constant reminder of your aspirations.

The power of visualization combined with SMART goals and the Pareto principle is a dynamic trio that can transform your dreams into reality. Visualize your success in intricate detail, set SMART goals that align with the Pareto principle, and craft a vision that ignites your passion and drives your actions. Remember, the journey to success is not just about reaching the destination but also about savoring every step of the adventure along the way.

Chapter 4: Applying Pareto in Time Management

4.1 Time as a Limited Resource

Time, as the saying goes, is money. But it's even more valuable than that. Time is the currency of life itself. It's the one resource that, once spent, can never be replenished. In this sub-chapter, we're going to explore the profound concept of time as a limited resource and how understanding this principle is the first step towards effective time management.

Understanding Time Constraints

Imagine you had a bank account with a fixed amount of money, and you couldn't deposit any more funds into it. Every day, you could only withdraw a certain amount. This bank account represents your time. You have 24 hours in a day, and you can't magically add more hours to it.

So, how do you spend this precious resource? Many people go through life as if their time were an unlimited wellspring. They fritter away minutes and hours on activities that don't bring them closer to their goals, both personal and professional. They fail to recognize that their time is finite and should be managed with care.

Successful individuals understand this fundamental truth and treat their time with the utmost respect. They become time-conscious, viewing each minute as an opportunity to invest in their future. They know that once a minute is gone, it's gone forever, along with the potential it held.

Identifying Time-Wasters

To make the most of your limited time, you must identify and eliminate time-wasting activities. These are the tasks that don't contribute significantly to your goals or well-being but consume a disproportionate amount of your time. They're the equivalent of financial investments that yield little to no return.

Common time-wasters include excessive social media scrolling, endless meetings that lack clear objectives, procrastination, and indulging in unproductive habits. Think of these activities as the weeds in your time garden. Left unchecked, they can overrun your schedule and suffocate your productivity.

Here's a simple exercise to identify your time-wasters: Keep a time log for a week. Write down how you spend every minute of your day. At the end of the week, review your log and highlight activities that didn't contribute meaningfully to your goals. These are your time-wasters.

Once you've identified them, you can take steps to minimize or eliminate them. For instance, limit your social media use to specific times of the day, set clear meeting agendas, and adopt techniques like the Pomodoro method to beat procrastination.

The 80/20 Rule in Daily Schedules

Now that you understand the concept of time as a finite resource and have identified your time-wasters, it's time to introduce you to a game-changer: the 80/20 rule, also known as the Pareto Principle.

The 80/20 rule states that roughly 80% of your results come from 20% of your efforts. In the context of time management, it means that a small portion of your activities yield the majority of your desired outcomes. Conversely, a significant portion of your activities has minimal impact.

To apply the 80/20 rule effectively to your daily schedule, start by identifying the 20% of activities that contribute the most to your goals and well-being. These are your high-value tasks. They might include activities like focused work on important projects, networking with key contacts, exercising, or spending quality time with loved ones.

Once you've identified your high-value tasks, prioritize them in your daily schedule. Allocate the best part of your day—the time when you're most focused and energized—to these tasks. This ensures that you're dedicating your peak performance hours to activities that generate the most significant results.

By following the 80/20 rule, you're not only optimizing your time management but also aligning your efforts with the most critical aspects of your life. It's a simple yet powerful strategy that can transform your daily schedule from a chaotic jumble of tasks to a well-orchestrated symphony of productivity.

Time is a limited resource that demands careful management. Understanding the constraints of time, identifying and eliminating time-wasters, and applying the 80/20 rule in your daily schedule are key steps in mastering the art of time management. Remember, your time is your most precious asset—spend it wisely, and you'll unlock the door to greater productivity and success.

4.2 The Pareto Productivity System

In the hustle and bustle of our modern lives, we often find ourselves juggling an overwhelming number of tasks, obligations, and responsibilities. It can be easy to feel like we're constantly running on a hamster wheel, exerting immense effort but making minimal progress. That's where the Pareto Productivity System comes to the rescue. This dynamic approach to time management harnesses the power of the Pareto principle to help you achieve more with less effort.

Prioritizing Tasks Effectively

Imagine your to-do list as a buffet table filled with various dishes of different sizes and flavors. Some tasks are small, while others are substantial and time-consuming. The key to effective time management is understanding that not all tasks are created equal. To truly excel in the art of productivity, you must learn the delicate skill of prioritization.

1. Identifying High-Impact Tasks: The first step in prioritizing effectively is recognizing which tasks have the

greatest impact on your goals. These tasks are the 20% that yield 80% of your desired outcomes. By focusing your energy and attention on them, you can create a domino effect that propels you toward success.

   - **Key Point 1: Identifying High-Impact Tasks**: Start by evaluating your to-do list. Which tasks are most closely aligned with your objectives? These are your high-impact tasks. They might not always be the most urgent, but they are the ones that will move the needle.

2. Urgency vs. Importance: It's easy to get caught up in the urgency of daily tasks—the phone calls, emails, and meetings that demand immediate attention. However, not everything that's urgent is necessarily important. Pareto's wisdom encourages us to distinguish between the two and allocate our resources accordingly.

   - **Key Point 2: Distinguishing Urgency from Importance**: Consider the long-term consequences of each task. Urgent tasks may require your immediate attention, but important tasks contribute significantly to your overall objectives. Strive to strike a balance.

3. The Eisenhower Matrix: One helpful tool for prioritization is the Eisenhower Matrix, which categorizes tasks into four quadrants based on their urgency and importance.

   - **Key Point 3: The Eisenhower Matrix**:

- Quadrant 1: Urgent and Important (Do immediately)

- Quadrant 2: Not Urgent but Important (Schedule and prioritize)

- Quadrant 3: Urgent but Not Important (Delegate if possible)

- Quadrant 4: Neither Urgent nor Important (Eliminate or minimize)

By taking a strategic approach to task prioritization, you can allocate your time and energy where it matters most, ensuring that you're consistently working on activities that drive you toward your goals.

Time Blocking and Focus

Once you've identified your high-impact tasks, the next step in the Pareto Productivity System is to allocate dedicated time blocks for these activities. Time blocking is a powerful technique that helps you structure your day for maximum efficiency.

1. The Magic of Time Blocking: Time blocking involves setting aside specific blocks of time on your calendar for focused work on a particular task or category of tasks. During these blocks, you commit to giving your full attention to the task at hand.

- **Key Point 1: Setting Time Blocks**: Start by identifying the best times of day for your high-impact tasks. Allocate uninterrupted time blocks for deep work and concentration.

Protect these time blocks as you would any other important appointment.

2. Minimizing Distractions: In our hyper-connected world, distractions are everywhere. Social media, notifications, and the constant ping of incoming emails can derail your focus in an instant. To make the most of your time blocks, it's essential to minimize distractions.

   - **Key Point 2: Creating a Distraction-Free Zone**: Find a quiet, comfortable workspace where you can concentrate without interruptions. Consider using website blockers or productivity apps to limit access to distracting websites during your focused work time.

3. The Pomodoro Technique: For those who find it challenging to maintain focus for extended periods, the Pomodoro Technique can be a game-changer. It involves working in short, focused bursts (typically 25 minutes) followed by a short break.

   - **Key Point 3: Implementing the Pomodoro Technique**: Set a timer for 25 minutes and commit to working on your task with unwavering focus during that time. After each Pomodoro session, reward yourself with a 5-minute break. Rinse and repeat.

Time blocking combined with a commitment to minimizing distractions and implementing focus-enhancing techniques can significantly boost your productivity and help you accomplish more in less time. This systematic approach ensures that you're making the most of your high-impact tasks.

Streamlining Workflows for Efficiency

Efficiency is the secret sauce that makes the Pareto Productivity System truly shine. Once you've prioritized your tasks and allocated focused time blocks, the final piece of the puzzle is streamlining your workflows.

1. Optimizing Processes: Take a close look at how you approach your tasks. Are there repetitive steps that can be automated or streamlined? Pareto's principle encourages us to identify the vital few actions that lead to the majority of results.

   - **Key Point 1: The Power of Automation**: Explore tools and technologies that can automate routine tasks. Whether it's email filters, task management apps, or marketing automation, these tools can free up valuable time.

2. Batching Similar Tasks: Another efficiency-boosting technique is task batching. Instead of switching between different types of tasks throughout the day, group similar tasks together and tackle them in one go.

   - **Key Point 2: Task Batching**: For example, if you have multiple emails to respond to, set aside a specific time block for email communication. Batching not only saves time but also reduces mental switching costs.

3. Continuous Improvement: The Pareto Productivity System is not a one-size-fits-all solution. It's a dynamic approach that encourages continuous improvement. Regularly assess your processes and workflows to identify areas where further efficiency gains can be made.

   - **Key Point 3: Kaizen—The Art of Continuous Improvement**: Embrace the Japanese philosophy of Kaizen, which emphasizes small, incremental improvements over time. By consistently seeking ways to optimize your work, you can achieve remarkable results.

Incorporating these principles of streamlining and efficiency into your daily routine can revolutionize how you manage your time and tasks. The Pareto Productivity System, with its focus on the vital few, time blocking, and workflow optimization, empowers you to achieve more while expending less effort.

Remember, the goal is not to fill every moment of your day with activity but to strategically allocate your time and energy to tasks that drive meaningful progress. By mastering the Pareto Productivity System, you'll unlock the potential to accomplish your goals with greater ease and efficiency, setting the stage for success in all areas of your life.

4.3 Achieving Work-Life Balance

In our fast-paced, modern world, achieving work-life balance often feels like chasing a mirage on a never-ending horizon. With mounting responsibilities, demanding careers, and an ever-expanding to-do list, it's easy to lose sight of the need to allocate time for our personal lives. But fret not, my friend, because the Pareto principle can come to your rescue once again, helping you reclaim the equilibrium between your professional and personal domains.

Allocating Time for Personal Life

Imagine a life where your personal life isn't an afterthought but a cherished and nurtured part of your daily routine. Pareto reminds us that 20% of our efforts can yield 80% of our desired outcomes, which means that carving out quality time for your personal life doesn't require Herculean efforts. It's all about smart, strategic allocation.

Start by examining your daily schedule. Identify the tasks and activities that consume most of your time, and ask yourself if they truly align with your personal priorities. Many of us fall into the trap of allowing work to seep into every crevice of our lives, but it doesn't have to be that way.

Prioritize the critical tasks in your work life that truly drive results, and ruthlessly eliminate or delegate the rest. This leaves you with more time to allocate to your personal life, whether it's spending quality moments with loved ones, pursuing hobbies, or simply relaxing.

One effective technique is time blocking. Designate specific time slots in your schedule exclusively for personal activities. Treat these appointments with yourself as non-negotiable, just as you would with important work meetings. Whether it's an hour of daily exercise, a weekly date night with your partner, or a weekend getaway with family, these blocks become the cornerstone of your balanced life.

Remember, it's not about the quantity of personal time but the quality. Cherish and savor these moments, and you'll find that the joy they bring spills over into other aspects of your life, enhancing your overall well-being.

Avoiding Exhaustion with Pareto

Exhaustion, that relentless foe of productivity and happiness, often creeps up when we least expect it. But fret not; Pareto offers a potent antidote. By understanding that not all tasks are created equal, you can stave off burnout and preserve your mental and physical health.

Identify the tasks that drain you the most, those that seem to gobble up your time with little reward. These are the culprits responsible for burnout. Apply the 80/20 rule to your daily work, and focus on the 20% of tasks that deliver 80% of the results. This not only reduces your workload but also prevents the feeling of spinning your wheels.

Another vital aspect of avoiding exhaustion is setting boundaries. Many of us feel the pressure to be available around the clock, thanks to the constant connectivity of our digital age. But remember that your time is precious, and you're entitled to protect it.

Consider establishing digital boundaries, such as turning off work-related notifications outside of business hours. Let your colleagues and superiors know your designated response times, and ensure that you have uninterrupted personal time to recharge and rejuvenate.

Pareto also encourages delegation. Recognize that you don't have to be a one-person show. Empower your team or colleagues by entrusting them with tasks that align with their strengths. By doing so, you not only reduce your workload but also foster a sense of collaboration and shared responsibility.

Sustaining Long-Term Productivity
Sustainability is key to maintaining a work-life balance that withstands the test of time. It's not just about finding momentary reprieve; it's about creating a lifestyle that sustains your well-being and productivity in the long run.

Think of your life as a marathon, not a sprint. Pareto teaches us that consistency often trumps intensity. Instead of sporadic bursts of productivity followed by burnout, aim for a steady, manageable pace. This involves setting realistic goals and expectations, both in your professional and personal life.

One powerful technique is time batching. Group similar tasks together and tackle them during designated time blocks. This minimizes the cognitive load of constantly switching between different types of work, making you more efficient and less fatigued.

Additionally, embrace the concept of "strategic laziness." Yes, you read that right. This means deliberately allowing yourself downtime without guilt. It's during these moments of relaxation that your mind has the opportunity to recharge and spark creative insights.

Remember, you're not a machine. You need rest, and you deserve it. Pareto reminds us that the 80/20 principle extends to rest and recovery as well. Just as 20% of your efforts can yield 80% of your results, 20% of your downtime can rejuvenate you for 80% of your tasks.

Achieving work-life balance isn't an elusive dream; it's a tangible reality within your grasp. The Pareto principle equips you with the tools to allocate time wisely, avoid burnout, and sustain productivity over the long haul. By embracing these principles and weaving them into the fabric of your daily life, you can create a harmonious existence where both work and personal fulfillment flourish.

Chapter 5: Prioritizing Your Efforts for Maximum Impact

5.1 The Art of Prioritization

In the quest for success, few skills are as indispensable as the art of prioritization. It's the compass that guides us through the labyrinth of tasks and responsibilities, ensuring that we invest our precious time and energy where they matter most. In this sub-chapter, we'll dive deep into the intricacies of prioritization, discovering how the Pareto principle can be a beacon of light in the often tumultuous sea of choices and commitments.

Identifying Your Highest-Value Activities

Imagine your day as a vast landscape with countless hills and valleys. Some tasks are towering peaks, while others are mere foothills. Your highest-value activities are those majestic peaks—the ones that, when conquered, have the greatest impact on your journey toward success.

Identifying these activities is the first step on your path to prioritization mastery. It's about recognizing the tasks that align most closely with your goals, values, and long-term vision. These are the activities that, when accomplished, propel you forward with the force of a rocket.

But how do you distinguish the peaks from the foothills? Begin by taking stock of your goals. What are you trying to achieve in your career, relationships, health, and personal development? What values drive you at your core?

For instance, if your goal is to become a renowned writer, then the act of writing itself is a high-value activity. It's your pen-to-paper time that shapes your destiny. Conversely, spending hours endlessly scrolling through social media may feel productive, but it's more likely a foothill, offering little progress toward your literary aspirations.

One powerful technique is to keep a journal of your daily activities for a week or two. Note how much time you devote to each task and evaluate its impact on your goals. You'll quickly identify patterns and opportunities for improvement. Remember, not all tasks are created equal; some are like seeds that, when planted, grow into mighty oaks.

Pareto-Driven Decision Making
Once you've identified your highest-value activities, the next step is to make decisions that align with these priorities. This is where the Pareto principle, with its 80/20 magic, can work wonders.

Imagine you're a manager with a team of ten employees. It's likely that 20% of your team members are responsible for 80% of the results. By recognizing this, you can focus your attention and resources on those high-performing individuals, thus maximizing your team's overall productivity.

Pareto-driven decision making is about making choices that yield the greatest returns. It's the realization that not all efforts have equal impact. In fact, many tasks are just noise, distracting you from your true mission.

To put this into practice, start by assessing your to-do list. Which tasks fall into the 20% category—the ones that will generate 80% of your desired outcomes? These are your priority tasks. Give them the spotlight of your attention, and delegate or minimize the others as much as possible.

For example, if you're an entrepreneur launching a new product, focus on the core features that will make or break its success. Pour your resources into refining these features and marketing them effectively. The less critical features can be addressed later, once your flagship product is thriving.

Balancing Urgency and Importance
In the journey of life, urgency often screams for our immediate attention. It's the blaring alarm clock that insists we act now, whether it's responding to emails, handling urgent client requests, or fixing a leaking roof. While these tasks may demand our immediate attention, they don't necessarily correlate with importance.

This is where the Eisenhower Matrix can be a lifesaver. President Dwight D. Eisenhower, known for his exceptional time management skills, famously said, "What is important is seldom urgent, and what is urgent is seldom important."

The matrix divides tasks into four categories:

1. Urgent and Important: These are tasks that demand immediate attention and align with your highest-value activities. They're the fires that must be put out to prevent catastrophe.

2. Not Urgent but Important: This quadrant is the heart of your prioritization strategy. These tasks may not scream for attention, but they have the potential to transform your life. It's where you invest time in your personal growth, long-term planning, and relationship-building.

3. Urgent but Not Important: These are the deceptive tasks that appear urgent but have little long-term impact. They often involve reacting to others' demands or crises that don't align with your goals.

4. Not Urgent and Not Important: The final quadrant is where distractions reside. These tasks neither demand immediate attention nor contribute to your goals. They're the time-wasters, the black holes of productivity.

To truly master the art of prioritization, strive to spend more time in quadrant 2—focusing on tasks that are important but not necessarily urgent. These are the activities that pave the road to your desired destination. Reserve quadrant 1 for genuine emergencies, minimize quadrant 3 where possible, and eliminate quadrant 4 entirely.

For instance, suppose you're a student working toward a degree. While completing assignments and attending lectures might fall into quadrant 1, dedicating time each day to study, research, and long-term project planning (quadrant 2) will yield the greatest academic success over time.

In essence, prioritization is the art of balancing the urgency of the moment with the importance of the task. It's about recognizing that what's important may not always be urgent, and vice versa. By applying the Pareto principle and the wisdom of the Eisenhower Matrix, you'll become a masterful conductor of your life's orchestra, ensuring that every note played contributes to a harmonious and fulfilling symphony of success.

5.2 Pareto in Project Management

In the world of self-help and personal development, we often focus on optimizing our individual efforts to achieve success. But what if I told you that these principles can be applied not only to your personal life but also to the projects and tasks you undertake? In this sub-chapter, we'll dive deep into the application of the Pareto principle in project management, a domain where efficiency and effectiveness are paramount.

Efficient Resource Allocation

Picture this: You're managing a project, and you have a limited pool of resources at your disposal – time, manpower, and budget. The conventional approach might be to distribute these resources evenly across all project components. However, Pareto teaches us to think differently. It suggests that a small portion of the effort can yield a disproportionately large impact.

1. Identifying Key Tasks: The first step in applying Pareto to project management is to identify the critical tasks that will have the most significant impact on project success. These tasks are often referred to as the "vital few." By focusing on them, you can maximize the efficiency of your resource allocation.

Imagine you're building a new product. Identifying the key features that will make or break the product's success is crucial. Allocating a significant portion of your resources to developing these features ensures that you're investing where it matters most.

2. Prioritizing Resource Allocation: Once you've identified the vital few tasks, it's time to allocate your resources wisely. Instead of spreading resources evenly across all project aspects, concentrate them on the critical tasks. This approach ensures that you're putting your efforts where they will make the most significant impact.

Think of it as a gardener tending to their garden. Rather than watering every plant equally, they focus on the plants that need it the most, resulting in healthier and more robust growth.

3. Resource Optimization: Pareto in project management isn't just about allocating resources efficiently; it's also about optimizing them. When you concentrate your efforts on the vital few tasks, you can apply your resources more effectively, leading to higher quality outcomes and faster progress.

Consider a construction project. By prioritizing the critical phases, such as laying the foundation and erecting the structural frame, you can expedite the project's timeline and reduce the risk of delays.

Risk Mitigation with Pareto

Every project comes with its fair share of risks and uncertainties. In traditional project management, the focus is often on identifying and addressing all potential risks, leading to exhaustive risk registers and contingency plans. However, Pareto encourages us to approach risk mitigation more strategically.

1. Identifying Critical Risks: Instead of spreading your attention thin across all potential risks, Pareto suggests that you focus on identifying the critical risks – those that could have the most severe consequences. These are the risks that, if left unaddressed, could derail your project.

Think of it as a chess game. While it's essential to consider all possible moves, a skilled player spends more time analyzing the moves that pose the greatest threat to their victory.

2. Proactive Risk Management: Once you've pinpointed the critical risks, it's time to take proactive measures to mitigate them. Pareto encourages us to allocate a significant portion of our risk management efforts to these high-impact risks.

For instance, if you're planning an outdoor event and weather conditions could make or break its success, you'd allocate extra resources to monitoring weather forecasts and implementing contingency plans for adverse weather.

3. Efficient Contingency Planning: Pareto also emphasizes efficiency in contingency planning. Rather than creating extensive backup plans for every conceivable scenario, focus on the most critical risks and develop targeted, effective mitigation strategies for them.

In the world of technology, this could mean investing in robust data backup systems and cybersecurity measures to protect against the most significant threats, ensuring that even in the face of adversity, your project can continue without major disruptions.

Meeting Project Deadlines
In today's fast-paced world, meeting project deadlines is non-negotiable. However, many projects struggle with delays, causing frustration and potential financial setbacks. Pareto can be your guiding star in ensuring timely project completion.

1. Identifying Critical Milestones: When managing a project, it's essential to identify critical milestones – key points in the project timeline that, if met, keep the project on track. Pareto encourages you to focus your efforts on these milestones, as they have the most substantial impact on the overall project deadline.

Think of it as a cross-country road trip. While there may be numerous interesting stops along the way, it's essential to prioritize reaching your destination by a certain date. These milestones are your checkpoints for progress.

2. Efficient Task Sequencing: Another crucial aspect of meeting project deadlines is sequencing tasks efficiently. Pareto suggests that you allocate more time and resources to tasks that are on the critical path, meaning they directly impact the project's timeline.

Consider building a complex piece of machinery. Ensuring that the most critical components are manufactured and assembled first ensures that any unexpected delays in those stages won't cascade into missed deadlines.

3. Continuous Monitoring and Adaptation: Pareto's principles don't stop at the planning stage. They extend into project execution. Continuously monitor the progress of critical milestones and adjust your resources and efforts as needed to keep the project on schedule.

Think of it as sailing a ship towards a distant island. Constantly adjusting your sails to harness the wind efficiently ensures you reach your destination as planned, even if you encounter unexpected currents.

By applying Pareto in project management, you'll not only enhance the efficiency of your resource allocation, but you'll also become a master of risk mitigation and deadline management. These principles, when embraced, can lead to successful project outcomes, reduced stress, and a reputation for delivering results. Remember, it's not about doing more; it's about doing what matters most.

5.3 Personal Prioritization Techniques

In the relentless hustle and bustle of modern life, we often find ourselves overwhelmed by an ever-growing list of tasks and responsibilities. Whether you're an ambitious professional, a dedicated parent, or a passionate entrepreneur, the demands on your time and energy can feel endless. In this sub-chapter, we're going to delve into the art of personal prioritization, a key component of the Pareto principle that can help you achieve maximum impact with minimum effort.

Pareto-Driven To-Do Lists

Let's face it—most of us are familiar with the concept of to-do lists. We scribble down our tasks, whether on paper or digitally, with the hope that this will help us stay organized and efficient. But have you ever considered how to transform your to-do list into a powerful tool for productivity using the Pareto principle?

Key Point 1: Pareto-Driven To-Do Lists

Imagine for a moment that your to-do list is not just a random collection of tasks but a carefully curated selection of items that align with the 80/20 rule. Here's how you can do it:

1. Identify the Vital Few: Start by distinguishing the 20% of tasks that will yield 80% of your desired results. These are your "vital few." They could be high-impact work assignments, important personal goals, or tasks that align with your long-term vision.

2. Eliminate or Delegate the Trivial Many: Now, take a critical look at the remaining 80% of tasks—the "trivial many." Can some of them be eliminated altogether? Are there tasks that can be delegated to others? By doing so, you free up your valuable time and energy for what truly matters.

3. Prioritize and Sequence: Arrange your tasks in a logical sequence that allows you to transition smoothly from one to the next. Prioritize them based on urgency, importance, and their potential to create a domino effect of productivity.

4. Focus on Completion, Not Just Activity: As you work through your to-do list, focus on completing tasks rather than simply being busy. The satisfaction of crossing items off your list will motivate you to keep going.

Key Point 2: The Power of Pareto-Driven To-Do Lists

The magic of Pareto-driven to-do lists lies in their ability to ensure that your efforts are channeled towards activities that truly move the needle. You'll experience a sense of accomplishment as you consistently tackle high-impact tasks, leading to increased productivity and reduced stress.

Imagine, for instance, that you're an entrepreneur launching a new product. Rather than spending hours on low-impact tasks like checking emails or tweaking minor design elements, you focus your energy on activities like market research, customer feedback, and marketing strategies. By aligning your efforts with the vital few, you're more likely to achieve success with less effort.

Focus on Your Strengths

While it's essential to prioritize tasks, it's equally important to recognize and leverage your strengths. Your strengths are the unique talents, skills, and attributes that set you apart from others. When you harness them effectively, you can maximize your impact in both your personal and professional life.

Key Point 1: Embracing Your Strengths

Embracing your strengths begins with self-awareness. Take the time to reflect on what you excel at and what brings you joy. Your strengths may include problem-solving, creativity, empathy, leadership, or a combination of various skills. These are your superpowers, waiting to be unleashed.

Key Point 2: Aligning Tasks with Your Strengths

Once you've identified your strengths, align your tasks and responsibilities with them. For example, if you're a natural communicator, focus on roles or projects that involve public speaking, writing, or networking. If you're highly analytical, seek out tasks that require data analysis, strategy development, or complex problem-solving.

Key Point 3: Delegating or Outsourcing Weaknesses

While it's important to leverage your strengths, it's equally crucial to acknowledge your weaknesses. We all have areas where we may not excel. Instead of struggling with tasks that fall outside your skill set, consider delegating or outsourcing them to others who specialize in those areas. This not only saves you time but also ensures a higher quality outcome.

Key Point 4: Continuous Growth and Skill Development

While focusing on your strengths is essential, it doesn't mean you should neglect areas where you have potential for growth. Continuous learning and skill development can expand your repertoire and make you more versatile. However, be mindful not to spread yourself too thin; prioritize growth in areas that align with your long-term goals.

Saying No Strategically

In a world filled with opportunities and obligations, the ability to say no strategically can be a game-changer. Many of us struggle with the fear of disappointing others or missing out on potential benefits, leading to an overloaded schedule and diminished effectiveness. However, mastering the art of saying no can be liberating.

Key Point 1: The Power of Strategic No's

Saying no strategically is not about being negative or uncooperative. It's about setting boundaries and preserving your time and energy for what truly matters. Here's how you can harness the power of strategic no's:

1. Assess Your Priorities: Before committing to a new task or obligation, evaluate whether it aligns with your priorities and long-term goals. If it doesn't, it's a prime candidate for a strategic no.

2. Practice Clarity and Honesty: When declining an opportunity, be clear and honest about your reasons. You don't need to offer a lengthy explanation, but a polite and straightforward response can help others understand your decision.

3. Offer Alternatives: If possible, suggest alternatives or compromises that might still provide value to the other party. This demonstrates your willingness to collaborate while maintaining your boundaries.

4. Learn to Say No Gracefully: Saying no doesn't have to be confrontational. You can say it gracefully by expressing appreciation for the opportunity and explaining your current commitments or limitations.

Key Point 2: The Freedom of Strategic No's

Strategic no's liberate you from the shackles of overcommitment and allow you to focus on what truly matters. When you say no to distractions, you make room for the vital few—the activities that align with your goals and aspirations. This leads to increased productivity, reduced stress, and a greater sense of control over your life.

Consider this scenario: You're already managing a demanding project at work, and a colleague asks you to take on an additional, less critical task. Instead of automatically saying yes, you assess your current workload and recognize that this new task would only divert your attention from the project's success. By strategically saying no, you protect your ability to excel in your primary responsibilities.

Personal prioritization techniques are the foundation of a Pareto-driven lifestyle. By curating your to-do lists, focusing on your strengths, and strategically saying no, you'll discover a newfound sense of control and efficiency in your life. Remember that these techniques are not just about doing less; they're about doing what matters most. As you integrate them into your daily routine, you'll find yourself achieving more with less effort, ultimately leading to a life filled with purpose and fulfillment.

Chapter 6: Pareto in Business and Career Advancement

6.1 Pareto in Business Strategy

In the relentless race towards success in the world of business, one principle reigns supreme: Pareto's 80/20 rule. It's not just a statistical phenomenon; it's a strategic goldmine waiting to be unearthed. In this sub-chapter, we'll delve into the dynamic world of business strategy, where the Pareto principle isn't just a theory; it's the blueprint for domination.

Identifying High-Value Customers

Let's start with the beating heart of any business: the customers. It's no secret that not all customers are created equal. Some bring a torrent of revenue, while others merely trickle in. This is where Pareto's magic comes into play.

Picture your customer base as a vast ocean, teeming with fish of all sizes. The 80/20 rule tells us that 20% of those fish will yield 80% of your catch. In business, this means that a select group of customers will contribute the lion's share of your profits. Your task is to identify them.

Key Point 1: Identifying the Golden 20%

Start by analyzing your customer data. Who are the clients that consistently bring in the most revenue? What industries do they belong to? Where are they located? What products or services do they favor?

By drilling down into the specifics, you'll unearth the gems amidst the gravel. These high-value customers are your lifeblood, and catering to their needs should be your priority. Tailor your marketing efforts, customer service, and product development to keep them satisfied and engaged.

Streamlining Business Processes
Once you've identified your high-value customers, it's time to optimize your operations. Think of your business processes as a well-oiled machine. Efficiency isn't a luxury; it's a necessity.

Pareto's wisdom teaches us that not all tasks and processes are equally important. Some contribute significantly to your bottom line, while others are mere distractions. Your goal is to streamline operations by focusing on the critical few.

Key Point 1: Process Evaluation

Conduct a comprehensive review of your business processes. Which steps are essential for delivering value to your high-value customers, and which are redundant or low-impact? Map out your processes, and identify bottlenecks and inefficiencies.

Key Point 2: Eliminating Waste

Now comes the challenging part - eliminating waste. Pareto tells us that 80% of results come from 20% of efforts. This means that you can cut out the excess, freeing up resources, time, and energy.

Empower your team to brainstorm and implement process improvements. Encourage a culture of continuous improvement where everyone is vested in the quest for efficiency. Over time, this will not only reduce costs but also enhance your ability to serve your top-tier customers.

Key Point 3: Leveraging Technology for Efficiency

In the digital age, technology is your ally in achieving Pareto-inspired efficiency. Automation, data analytics, and cloud computing are just a few tools at your disposal. Invest in technology that supports your high-value customers and simplifies your operations.

Maximizing Profit Margins
In the realm of business strategy, profit margins are the compass that guides your ship. Every decision, every move should ultimately lead to the holy grail of profitability. With the Pareto principle as your guide, you can navigate these treacherous waters with confidence.

Key Point 1: Pricing Strategies

Price is one of the most potent levers in your profit-maximizing toolkit. Pareto suggests that a small portion of your products or services generate the majority of your profits. These are your premium offerings.

Identify your high-profit products or services and position them strategically. Consider value-based pricing for these items, ensuring that you capture the maximum value from your customers. Don't be afraid to adjust prices in response to market conditions and customer feedback.

Key Point 2: Cost Optimization

Every dollar saved is a dollar earned, as the saying goes. Pareto reminds us that not all expenses are created equal. Some expenses are vital to maintaining your business, while others are discretionary. Identify areas where cost optimization is possible without compromising quality or service.

Engage your team in cost-saving initiatives, and reward innovation that leads to lower costs. Keep a watchful eye on your supply chain, renegotiate contracts when feasible, and explore opportunities for bulk purchasing or economies of scale.

Key Point 3: Diversification and Innovation

Diversification and innovation can be potent tools for increasing profit margins. Pareto doesn't advocate putting all your eggs in one basket; it encourages you to identify the most profitable ones.

Explore opportunities to expand your product or service offerings in alignment with the preferences of your high-value customers. But remember, innovation doesn't mean reckless expansion. Each new venture should be scrutinized through the lens of Pareto to ensure it aligns with your core profit-generating activities.

In the intricate dance of business strategy, Pareto's principle is your trusted partner. It helps you identify the gems among the stones, streamline your operations, and maximize your profit margins. By weaving these principles into your business tapestry, you'll not only succeed but thrive in the competitive world of commerce.

6.2 Career Advancement and Pareto

In the long journey of life, your career is a prominent thread that weaves through the fabric of your existence. It's not just about a job; it's about growth, fulfillment, and reaching your true potential. As we dive deeper into the world of Pareto and career advancement, you'll discover how to excel in your professional journey with the wisdom of the 80/20 rule.

Focusing on Key Skills

Imagine your career as a garden. To flourish, it needs the right nutrients, care, and attention. In the realm of career advancement, the Pareto principle reminds us that not all skills are created equal. Some skills are like the vibrant flowers in your garden, while others are the sturdy branches providing structure. Here's how to nurture your career garden effectively:

1: Identifying Your Key Skills

Your journey to career advancement begins with self-awareness. Take a moment to reflect on your strengths and weaknesses. What are the skills that set you apart? What do you excel at? These are your key skills—the flowers that deserve the most attention.

Pareto suggests that 20% of your skills contribute to 80% of your success. Identify that 20%. It could be your exceptional problem-solving abilities, your knack for leadership, or your proficiency in a particular technology. Once you've pinpointed your key skills, it's time to invest in them.

2: Skill Development and Improvement

Now that you've recognized your key skills, it's time to nurture them. Consider it like tending to the flowers in your garden. To make them bloom and thrive, you must feed them, water them, and protect them from pests.

In your career, this means investing time and effort into honing your skills. Take courses, attend workshops, and read books that relate to your key skills. Seek mentorship and guidance from experts in your field. The more you improve your key skills, the more valuable you become in your industry.

3: Delegating Non-Key Tasks

The Pareto principle also teaches us that the remaining 80% of tasks contribute to only 20% of our success. These are the non-key tasks—important but not as impactful as your core competencies. To excel in your career, consider delegating or outsourcing these tasks when possible.

Delegating frees up your time and energy to focus on what truly matters. If, for instance, your key skill is project management, delegate administrative tasks to an assistant. This way, you'll be able to allocate the majority of your time to tasks that leverage your strengths and propel your career forward.

Networking for Success

In the vast landscape of career advancement, your professional network acts as the fertile soil in which your career garden grows. Networking is not just about collecting business cards or LinkedIn connections; it's about nurturing meaningful relationships that can help you bloom. Let's delve into the art of networking with the Pareto perspective:

1: Quality Over Quantity

The 80/20 rule applies to networking as well. Instead of trying to connect with everyone you meet, focus on building deep and genuine relationships with the 20% of individuals who can make the most significant impact on your career.

These might be mentors who can guide you, colleagues who share your vision, or potential clients who believe in your expertise. Invest your time and effort in nurturing these connections, and you'll find that they yield the most fruitful results.

2: Giving Before Receiving

Effective networking is not just about what others can do for you; it's about how you can contribute to their success. Generosity breeds goodwill and trust, which are invaluable assets in any career.

When you meet someone in your field, ask yourself how you can help them. Maybe it's sharing your knowledge, providing a solution to their problem, or simply being a supportive ear. When you give without expecting immediate returns, you create a network that's built on authenticity and reciprocity.

3: Online and Offline Networking

Networking isn't limited to in-person events and meetings. In today's digital age, online networking plays a crucial role in career advancement. Platforms like LinkedIn, Twitter, and professional forums offer abundant opportunities to connect with like-minded individuals.

Use these platforms strategically. Share your insights, engage in discussions, and actively participate in online communities relevant to your field. By doing so, you'll not only expand your network but also position yourself as a thought leader—a valuable asset in career advancement.

Navigating Office Politics Efficiently
Office politics can sometimes feel like navigating a dense forest filled with hidden traps and unexpected challenges. However, understanding how to approach office politics with the Pareto perspective can help you maneuver through the corporate landscape more efficiently.

1: Observing and Understanding Dynamics

Before you jump into the fray of office politics, take a step back and observe the dynamics at play. Just as Pareto advises identifying the vital 20%, recognize the key players and influencers in your workplace. Who holds the most sway? What are the power structures at play?

Understanding these dynamics allows you to navigate office politics strategically. It's not about getting entangled in office drama but rather positioning yourself in a way that aligns with your career goals.

2: Building Positive Relationships

Office politics aren't inherently negative. They often involve building alliances and forming relationships that can be beneficial to your career. Focus on creating positive connections with colleagues and superiors.

Seek common ground, offer your assistance, and be a team player. By fostering a reputation for cooperation and collaboration, you'll find it easier to navigate office politics without getting caught in its negative aspects.

3: Staying True to Your Values

While it's essential to adapt and navigate office politics, never compromise your values or integrity. The Pareto principle reminds us that the most significant impact comes from authenticity and staying true to your core principles.

As you advance in your career, you'll encounter situations that challenge your ethics. In such moments, prioritize your values. The trust and credibility you maintain are far more valuable than any short-term gains from unethical behavior.

In the ever-evolving landscape of your career, embracing the Pareto principle can be your guiding light. By focusing on your key skills, nurturing meaningful relationships, and navigating office politics efficiently, you'll not only advance in your career but also find greater fulfillment and purpose in your professional journey.

6.3 Entrepreneurship and Pareto

In this subchapter, we dive into the world of entrepreneurship and discover how the Pareto principle can be your guiding star on the path to creating a successful business venture. Entrepreneurs are the modern-day pioneers, forging new paths, and taking calculated risks to bring their visions to life. In this age of innovation and opportunity, it's essential to leverage the power of Pareto to identify profitable ventures, allocate resources effectively, and scale your business for sustainable growth.

Identifying Profitable Ventures

Imagine you're standing at the crossroads of entrepreneurship, brimming with ideas and enthusiasm. You have a vision, but not all visions translate into profitable ventures. This is where Pareto can be your trusted companion.

1: Defining Your Niche

In the vast landscape of business possibilities, it's crucial to identify your niche, your sweet spot where your passion aligns with market demand. Pareto's wisdom reminds us that 20% of your efforts often yield 80% of your results. Apply this principle to your venture by focusing on the 20% of products, services, or ideas that have the potential to generate 80% of your profits.

To define your niche, ask yourself:

- What am I truly passionate about?

- Where does my expertise lie?

- Is there a demand for my offerings in the market?

- Who are my ideal customers?

2: Market Research and Validation

Pareto encourages us to be discerning and efficient. Instead of scattering your efforts in multiple directions, channel your energy into researching your niche thoroughly. Identify your competitors, study your target audience, and validate your business idea.

Market research doesn't have to be a cumbersome process. Pareto suggests that you can gather 80% of the critical information you need from 20% of your research efforts. Look for patterns, trends, and insights that can inform your business strategy.

3: The MVP Approach

Minimum Viable Product (MVP) is a concept deeply rooted in the entrepreneurial world. It's about launching your product or service with the minimum features required to satisfy early customers. Pareto's principle of prioritization plays a pivotal role here. Instead of investing all your resources in building a full-fledged product, focus on the critical 20% of features that will bring 80% of the value to your customers.

An MVP allows you to test the waters, gather user feedback, and make informed decisions based on real-world data. It's a lean and efficient way to ensure you're on the right track before committing significant resources.

Resource Allocation for Startups

Once you've identified a profitable venture, the next challenge is wisely allocating your resources. As an entrepreneur, your resources—be it time, money, or manpower—are limited. Pareto's principle becomes your guiding light in resource allocation.

1: Prioritizing Key Activities

Pareto's 80/20 rule applies here with even greater relevance. Identify the critical 20% of activities that will drive 80% of your business growth. These activities might include product development, marketing, customer acquisition, or strategic partnerships.

By concentrating your efforts on these key activities, you ensure that you're not spreading yourself too thin. This focused approach allows you to maximize your efficiency and impact.

2: Lean Budgeting

In the early stages of entrepreneurship, budgets can be tight. Pareto encourages you to adopt a lean budgeting strategy. Allocate your financial resources to the most critical areas of your business. This might mean outsourcing non-essential tasks, leveraging affordable software solutions, or bartering services with other entrepreneurs.

Remember that the 80/20 principle also applies to expenses. Analyze your costs and identify the 20% that contributes to 80% of your spending. Trim unnecessary expenses to optimize your budget.

3: Delegating and Outsourcing

Entrepreneurs often wear many hats, but Pareto advises against trying to do it all. Identify the tasks that require your unique skills and expertise—the vital 20%. Delegate or outsource the rest.

Delegating doesn't just save you time; it empowers others and fosters growth within your team. The 80/20 rule reminds us that by focusing on our strengths and letting go of non-essential tasks, we can achieve more with less effort.

Scaling Your Business with Pareto

Scaling a business is the dream of every entrepreneur. It's the phase where your initial efforts begin to compound, and growth accelerates. Pareto's wisdom can guide you through the scaling process efficiently and sustainably.

1: Identifying Scalable Elements

Not every aspect of your business is equally scalable. Pareto advises identifying the 20% of your business that can lead to 80% of your growth. This might involve pinpointing high-demand products or services, high-performing marketing channels, or key partnerships.

Scaling these elements first allows you to generate significant results with minimal additional effort.

2: Systems and Automation

As your business grows, manual processes can become bottlenecks. Pareto's principle encourages you to streamline and automate routine tasks. Look for opportunities to implement systems and technologies that can handle repetitive work efficiently.

The 80/20 rule also applies to customer segmentation. Identify the top 20% of your customers who contribute to 80% of your revenue. Tailor your marketing and customer service efforts to cater to their specific needs and preferences.

3: Monitoring and Adaptation

Pareto's philosophy isn't about set-it-and-forget-it; it's about continuous improvement. As you scale, regularly monitor your operations, and gather data. Identify the 20% of strategies and efforts that are delivering 80% of your results.

Be prepared to adapt and pivot. Scaling isn't a linear process; it's dynamic and often requires recalibrating your approach based on changing market conditions and customer feedback.

Entrepreneurship is a thrilling journey, and the Pareto principle can be your compass to navigate the challenging terrain of business and career advancement. By focusing on identifying profitable ventures, efficiently allocating resources, and scaling your business with Pareto's insights, you can build a thriving enterprise that not only succeeds but also thrives in the long run. Remember, success isn't just about working hard; it's about working smart, and Pareto's wisdom can help you do just that.

Chapter 7: Achieving Financial Success with Pareto

7.1 Pareto and Personal Finance

In the grand mosaic of life, our financial well-being plays a pivotal role. It can either act as a steadfast foundation, providing us with the freedom to pursue our dreams, or as a barrier, locking us into a never-ending cycle of financial stress. In this sub-chapter, we delve deep into the world of personal finance through the lens of the Pareto Principle. You're about to discover how the 80/20 rule can transform your financial landscape, making your money work smarter, not harder.

Smart Budgeting and Savings

Budgeting. It's a word that often evokes visions of spreadsheets and restrictions, but it doesn't have to be that way. With Pareto by your side, budgeting becomes an art form, a means of channeling your financial resources where they matter most.

1: Identifying the Vital 20%

Start your journey towards financial success by identifying the 20% of your expenses that account for 80% of your spending. This could include your housing costs, transportation expenses, and groceries. These are your "essential" expenses – the ones you can't do without. Begin by scrutinizing these categories.

Look for opportunities to optimize. Can you refinance your mortgage to lower your monthly payments? Is there a more fuel-efficient way to commute? Can you make smarter choices at the grocery store without sacrificing the quality of your meals?

By making small, strategic changes to these significant expenses, you can free up resources to invest in your financial future.

2: The Pareto Budgeting Technique

The Pareto Budgeting Technique is a powerful approach that helps you allocate your resources where they matter most. First, calculate your total monthly income. Next, prioritize your expenses. Start with the essential 20% – the categories we discussed earlier. Allocate a significant portion of your income to these expenses, ensuring they are covered comfortably.

Now comes the fun part. The remaining 80% of your income is split into two categories: the "Investment Fund" and the "Leisure Fund." The Investment Fund should receive a substantial portion of this 80%. This is where you'll allocate money for savings, investments, and paying off debt (more on that later).

The Leisure Fund is where you enjoy life's pleasures without guilt. Dining out, entertainment, and other discretionary spending fall into this category. By following this approach, you ensure your financial essentials are covered, while also directing a significant portion of your income toward building wealth.

3: Automate Your Finances

One of the secrets to success in personal finance is automation. Set up automatic transfers to your Investment Fund as soon as your paycheck lands in your account. This way, you're prioritizing your financial future without the temptation to spend the money elsewhere.

Furthermore, automate your bill payments to avoid late fees and maintain a stellar credit score. Embrace technology and personal finance apps to monitor your spending and savings effortlessly. By automating your finances, you ensure consistency in your financial habits, a key element in achieving long-term financial success.

Investment Strategies

Investing can feel like navigating a labyrinth, but with Pareto guiding you, it becomes a journey filled with purpose and potential. Here's how to apply the 80/20 rule to your investment strategy:

1: Focus on High-Yield Investments

The Pareto Principle tells us that not all investments are created equal. In fact, a small percentage of your investments will likely yield a significant portion of your returns. These are your "high-yield" investments.

Start by diversifying your investments across various asset classes, such as stocks, bonds, real estate, and even alternative investments like cryptocurrencies. However, within each asset class, prioritize high-yield options. These could be individual stocks with strong growth potential, bonds with higher interest rates, or real estate properties in emerging markets.

The key here is to allocate a majority of your investment capital to these high-yield opportunities. While they may carry more risk, they also offer the potential for substantial rewards.

2: Long-Term Perspective

The Pareto Principle teaches us the value of patience and long-term thinking. Apply this wisdom to your investment strategy by adopting a buy-and-hold approach. Avoid the temptation to constantly buy and sell investments in an attempt to time the market. Instead, focus on building a diversified portfolio of high-yield assets and let time work its magic.

Historically, the stock market has shown an upward trajectory over the long term, despite short-term fluctuations. By holding onto your investments for extended periods, you harness the power of compound returns, turning a small initial investment into substantial wealth over time.

3: Minimize Fees and Taxes

In the world of investing, fees and taxes can significantly erode your returns. Pareto principles come into play here as well. Identify the 20% of investments that generate 80% of your returns, and ensure that these are held in tax-efficient accounts.

Additionally, choose investment vehicles with lower fees and expenses. Index funds and exchange-traded funds (ETFs) often have lower costs compared to actively managed funds. By minimizing fees and taxes, you keep more of your returns, allowing your investments to grow at a faster rate.

Debt Management
Debt is a formidable adversary when it comes to financial success. However, the Pareto Principle can help you tackle it strategically.

1: Prioritize High-Interest Debt

Not all debt is created equal. Some debts, like credit card debt, carry exorbitant interest rates that can cripple your financial progress. Identify these high-interest debts as the 20% causing 80% of your financial stress.

Create a plan to aggressively pay down high-interest debts first. Allocate a significant portion of your Investment Fund to debt reduction until you've eliminated these high-cost obligations. This not only frees up more of your income for saving and investing but also provides peace of mind.

2: Leverage Low-Interest Debt

Not all debt is bad. In some cases, low-interest debt can be strategically used to your advantage. For instance, a mortgage with a favorable interest rate can allow you to build equity in real estate while maintaining liquidity for other investments.

Use the Pareto Principle to identify the low-interest debt that serves as the 20% providing 80% of your financial flexibility. Leverage such debt wisely to accelerate your wealth-building journey.

3: Debt Consolidation and Refinancing

Explore opportunities for debt consolidation and refinancing to optimize your debt management. By consolidating multiple high-interest loans into a single, lower-interest loan or refinancing high-interest mortgages, you can significantly reduce your interest costs.

Additionally, consider the impact of inflation. Over time, the real value of your debt decreases as prices rise. This can be especially advantageous for fixed-rate loans. With the right strategy, you can use inflation to your advantage, effectively reducing the burden of your debt.

Personal finance, when viewed through the lens of the Pareto Principle, becomes a journey of optimization and intentionality. By identifying the vital 20% of your expenses, prioritizing high-yield investments, and strategically managing debt, you pave the way for a financially abundant future. Remember, it's not about how much you earn; it's about how effectively you allocate and grow your resources. Your financial success story begins now, and with Pareto as your guide, the path.

7.2 Financial Independence and Pareto

In this sub-chapter, we're diving into a topic that resonates with almost everyone: financial independence. Who doesn't dream of a life where money isn't a constant worry, where you have the freedom to pursue your passions and interests without being tied to a 9-to-5 job? The Pareto principle, with its 80/20 rule, can be your trusted companion on the path to financial success and independence.

Building Passive Income Streams

Let's start with the idea of building passive income streams. Passive income is like the holy grail of financial success. It's money that flows in, month after month, with minimal effort on your part. To leverage the Pareto principle in this context, you need to identify the few income sources that generate the majority of your earnings.

1. Identifying High-Yield Ventures: Pareto advises us to focus on the most productive 20% of our efforts. In the world of finance, this means identifying the investments or

business ventures that yield the most return with the least effort.

For example, if you have a portfolio of stocks, you might find that a handful of them consistently outperform the others. By reallocating your resources into these top-performing stocks, you're maximizing your returns while reducing your overall effort and risk.

2. Diversification vs. Specialization: While diversification is a common strategy, Pareto challenges us to think differently. Instead of spreading your resources across many income sources, consider concentrating on a few key areas where you have expertise or where you see the most potential.

This might mean focusing on a specific niche if you're an entrepreneur or investing heavily in industries you understand well. By specializing, you're more likely to excel in those areas, increasing your chances of generating substantial passive income.

3. Automation and Delegation: Pareto's wisdom extends to automation and delegation. Once you've identified your most productive income sources, automate repetitive tasks and delegate responsibilities where possible. This frees up your time and mental energy to explore new opportunities or enjoy the fruits of your labor.

For instance, if you're earning rental income from properties, consider hiring a property management company to handle tenant issues and property maintenance. This allows you to benefit from the income while reducing the day-to-day involvement.

Retiring Early with Pareto Principles

Now, let's talk about retiring early – a dream that often seems out of reach for many. Retirement isn't about reaching a certain age; it's about achieving financial independence, where you have the choice to work or not. Pareto can help you retire early by focusing on the essential aspects of financial planning.

1. Savings and Investment: Pareto encourages us to scrutinize our savings and investments. Are you allocating your resources efficiently? Are there investment opportunities that could potentially accelerate your retirement timeline?

Consider the 80/20 rule when evaluating your investment portfolio. Are there specific assets or strategies that are contributing significantly to your growth? By reallocating your resources based on performance, you can maximize your returns and potentially retire earlier than you originally planned.

2. Living Below Your Means: Pareto's principle can also be applied to your lifestyle choices. In the quest for early

retirement, it's essential to minimize unnecessary expenses and focus on what truly matters.

Identify the 20% of your expenses that bring you 80% of your satisfaction and allocate your resources accordingly. This might mean cutting back on extravagant vacations or dining out less frequently while investing more in experiences that genuinely enrich your life.

3. Passive Income Strategies: Returning to the concept of passive income, early retirement often relies heavily on creating sustainable passive income streams. Pareto encourages you to examine which income sources are contributing most significantly to your financial independence.

Perhaps it's income from rental properties, dividends from a well-chosen portfolio of stocks, or royalties from intellectual property. By nurturing these income streams and continually seeking opportunities to optimize them, you can fast-track your path to retirement.

Achieving Financial Freedom
Financial freedom is the ultimate goal. It's not merely about accumulating wealth; it's about having the autonomy to make choices that align with your values and aspirations. The Pareto principle plays a pivotal role in achieving this freedom.

1. Goal Setting and Clarity: Pareto emphasizes the importance of clarity in goal setting. What does financial freedom look like to you? What are your specific objectives and timelines?

The 80/20 rule encourages you to focus on the most impactful actions that will propel you toward your financial freedom goals. This might mean honing your skills, identifying high-return investments, or developing a comprehensive financial plan.

2. Risk Management: Financial freedom often involves taking calculated risks. Pareto's principle urges you to analyze the risks and rewards of your financial decisions. What are the potential risks associated with your investments or entrepreneurial endeavors?

By concentrating on the most promising opportunities and mitigating risks where possible, you can confidently navigate the path to financial freedom.

3. Lifestyle Design: Finally, financial freedom allows you to design your ideal lifestyle. Pareto advises you to allocate your resources in a way that aligns with your values and aspirations. This might mean spending more time with loved ones, pursuing meaningful hobbies, or contributing to causes you're passionate about.

By leveraging the 80/20 principle, you can focus on the aspects of life that bring you the most joy and fulfillment while maintaining your financial stability.

The Pareto principle can become a practical guide to achieving financial independence and freedom. By identifying the most impactful actions, optimizing your income sources, and making intentional choices, you can pave the way for a future where financial worries are a thing of the past, and your dreams become your reality.

7.3 Philanthropy and Pareto

In the stages of life, there are few threads more beautiful than the one woven by philanthropy. The act of giving back not only enriches our communities but also nourishes our own souls. It's the realization that our success, in many ways, depends on the well-being of those around us. So, let's explore how the Pareto principle can amplify the impact of our philanthropic efforts, allowing us to maximize social good while continuing to thrive ourselves.

Strategic Charitable Giving

Charitable giving is a deeply personal choice, but it can also be a strategic one. The Pareto principle, with its 80/20 rule, offers valuable insights into how we can make our contributions count.

Consider this: 80% of the benefits often come from 20% of the efforts. In the realm of philanthropy, this means that a few carefully chosen charitable contributions can have a far-reaching impact compared to scattering donations across numerous causes.

So, how can you apply this principle to your charitable endeavors? Start by identifying the causes that resonate most with your values and passions. Perhaps it's education, healthcare, poverty alleviation, or environmental conservation. Once you've pinpointed these areas, research and select organizations that are not only aligned with your mission but also demonstrate a track record of efficiently utilizing donations.

Furthermore, consider the power of recurring donations. By consistently supporting a cause over time, you provide stability and allow organizations to plan for long-term initiatives. This sustained support can make a more significant impact than occasional large donations.

Remember, philanthropy is not just about giving money; it's about being actively engaged in the causes you care about. You can donate your time, skills, or resources to amplify your impact further. The key is to be intentional and strategic in your giving, ensuring that your contributions create a ripple effect of positive change.

Maximizing Social Impact
The Pareto principle extends beyond the allocation of resources; it also underscores the importance of focusing on

the most significant areas of need. When it comes to philanthropy, this means targeting the root causes of social issues rather than merely addressing their symptoms.

Imagine a garden plagued by weeds. One approach is to continually trim the visible weeds, which provides a temporary solution but doesn't address the underlying problem—the roots. The Pareto-inspired approach is to invest time and resources in uprooting the weeds at their source. By tackling the root causes, you create lasting change and prevent future issues from sprouting.

In the realm of philanthropy, this principle encourages us to support initiatives that aim to create systemic change. It means looking beyond immediate relief efforts and supporting organizations that focus on long-term solutions. For instance, if you're passionate about education, consider supporting programs that improve access to quality education for underserved communities rather than only funding short-term scholarships.

Moreover, collaboration is a powerful tool in maximizing social impact. By partnering with other philanthropists, organizations, and community leaders who share your goals, you can pool resources and expertise to tackle complex social challenges collectively.

Combining Success with Giving Back

One of the most beautiful aspects of philanthropy is that it's not limited to the ultra-wealthy. No matter where you are on your journey to financial success, there are opportunities to give back and make a difference.

As you navigate your path to success using Pareto's wisdom, consider integrating giving into your financial plan from the beginning. Set aside a percentage of your income for charitable contributions, just as you allocate funds for savings and investments. This proactive approach ensures that giving remains a consistent part of your financial life.

Additionally, think about creative ways to leverage your success for social good. If you're an entrepreneur, you can explore social enterprises, where profit and purpose coexist. By aligning your business goals with a social mission, you can make a positive impact while achieving financial success.

Furthermore, as you accumulate wealth and influence, consider using your voice and platform to advocate for causes that matter to you. Whether it's raising awareness about environmental conservation, championing social justice, or advocating for education reform, your influence can be a catalyst for change.

In the end, the Pareto principle reminds us that giving back is not only a responsibility but also a privilege. It's a way to create a positive legacy, to leave the world better than we found it. And as we combine our success with the art of strategic philanthropy, we can weave a thread of lasting impact into the fabric of our lives, making our journey truly remarkable.

Chapter 8: Using Pareto to Enhance Relationships

8.1 Pareto in Personal Relationships

In this sub-chapter, we delve into the intricate world of personal relationships, where the Pareto principle can be a game-changer. These relationships are the threads that weave the fabric of our lives, bringing warmth, joy, and sometimes, challenges. By applying the principles of Pareto, we can enhance the quality of these connections and create more fulfilling bonds.

Prioritizing Quality Time

In our fast-paced, modern world, it's easy to get caught up in the whirlwind of daily tasks and responsibilities. We often find ourselves juggling work, social commitments, and personal ambitions, leaving little room for the people we care about most. This is where the Pareto principle steps in, urging us to focus on what truly matters.

1: Reimagining Time Management

To prioritize quality time in your personal relationships, start by reimagining your approach to time management. Identify the 20% of activities that contribute to 80% of your relationship's happiness and well-being. These might include heartfelt conversations, shared experiences, or simply being present.

Allocate dedicated slots in your schedule for these essential moments. Treat them with the same level of importance you would a crucial work meeting or personal goal. By doing so, you'll ensure that your relationships receive the attention and care they deserve.

2: The Power of Presence

Quality time is not just about the quantity of minutes spent together but the quality of those moments. Being fully present when you're with loved ones is a gift you can give that holds immeasurable value. When you're engaged in a conversation or sharing an activity, put away distractions, such as your phone or work-related thoughts.

Listen actively and empathetically, allowing the other person to express themselves without judgment. This level of attentiveness fosters a deeper connection, as it communicates that you genuinely value and respect the relationship.

3: The Joy of Shared Experiences

Consider the activities that you and your loved ones enjoy doing together. These shared experiences often create lasting memories and strengthen the bond between you. Applying the Pareto principle here means identifying those experiences that bring the most joy and fulfillment.

It could be as simple as cooking a meal together, going for a hike, or attending a concert. Allocate more time and energy to these activities, and you'll find that your relationships thrive as a result. By doing less of what doesn't bring as much joy and more of what does, you'll build a stronger connection.

Communication Strategies

Effective communication is the cornerstone of any successful relationship, whether it's with a partner, family member, or friend. Applying the Pareto principle to communication involves recognizing the key elements that contribute to positive interactions and learning how to amplify their impact.

1: Active Listening and Empathy

Listening is an art that often goes underappreciated. In the hustle and bustle of our daily lives, we sometimes forget to truly listen to what others are saying. We're quick to jump in with our own opinions or thoughts, inadvertently diminishing the value of the exchange.

Pareto in personal relationships teaches us to identify the 20% of our communication that leads to 80% of understanding and connection. This often involves active listening, where you give your full attention to the speaker. Truly understanding their perspective and showing empathy can resolve conflicts and strengthen bonds.

2: Effective Expression

Communication is a two-way street, and while listening is crucial, expressing yourself effectively is equally important. Pareto encourages us to identify the 20% of our words and actions that contribute significantly to the quality of our relationships.

Consider the words you choose and the way you express yourself. Do they reflect your genuine feelings and intentions? Are they kind, respectful, and supportive? By focusing on these aspects, you can ensure that your communication enhances, rather than hinders, your relationships.

3: Conflict Resolution

Conflicts are a natural part of any relationship, but how we approach and resolve them can make all the difference. The Pareto approach to conflict resolution involves pinpointing the 20% of issues that cause 80% of the conflicts and addressing them proactively.

Instead of allowing small issues to escalate, focus on open and honest communication. Share your concerns calmly and respectfully, and encourage the other person to do the same. Seek common ground and compromise when necessary. By efficiently resolving conflicts, you'll create a healthier and more harmonious relationship.

Resolving Conflicts Efficiently

Conflict is not the enemy of relationships; unresolved conflict is. When handled effectively, conflict can lead to growth, understanding, and ultimately, a stronger bond. Pareto offers valuable insights into how to address and resolve conflicts efficiently.

1: Identifying Root Causes

Not all conflicts are created equal, and some may stem from deeper issues. The Pareto principle advises us to dig beneath the surface and identify the 20% of underlying causes that contribute to 80% of conflicts.

For example, recurring arguments about household chores might actually be rooted in a need for appreciation and respect. By recognizing these root causes, you can address the core issues and prevent future conflicts.

2: Constructive Communication

When conflicts arise, it's essential to approach them constructively. The Pareto mindset encourages us to focus on the 20% of communication strategies that yield 80% of conflict resolution success. These strategies include staying calm, avoiding blame, and actively seeking solutions.

Rather than dwelling on past grievances, focus on finding common ground and mutually beneficial solutions. Effective conflict resolution requires a willingness to compromise and a commitment to preserving the relationship.

3: Forgiveness and Moving Forward

Resolving conflicts efficiently also means knowing when to let go. Holding onto grudges and past mistakes can erode a relationship over time. Pareto in personal relationships teaches us that forgiveness is part of the 20% that leads to 80% of relationship healing.

Forgiveness doesn't mean condoning hurtful actions; it means choosing to release the negative emotions and move forward. By doing so, you free up mental and emotional space for a healthier, happier relationship.

Personal relationships are the tapestry of our lives, woven with threads of love, understanding, and connection. By applying the Pareto principle to these relationships, we can prioritize quality time, enhance communication, and resolve conflicts efficiently. Remember that the essence of any successful relationship lies in the 20% of effort that leads to 80% of the joy and fulfillment it brings.

8.2 Networking and Pareto

In today's interconnected world, the power of networking can hardly be overstated. It's often said that your network is your net worth, and this statement holds a profound truth. Networking isn't just about collecting business cards or LinkedIn connections; it's about building valuable relationships that can open doors to opportunities you might never have imagined. And when it comes to creating a network that truly works for you, the Pareto principle is your guiding star.

Building a Valuable Network

Imagine your network as a garden. Just as a gardener tends to their plants, you must cultivate and nurture your relationships. But here's where the Pareto principle comes into play: not all connections are created equal. In fact, a small percentage of your network will likely contribute the majority of your opportunities and support.

So, how can you apply the 80/20 rule to your networking efforts? Start by identifying your most valuable contacts. These are the individuals who consistently offer guidance, introductions, and genuine support. They're the ones who have a knack for being in the right place at the right time. Cultivate these relationships with care, as they are your key to unlocking a world of possibilities.

But don't stop there. Remember that the Pareto principle works in reverse as well; a small percentage of your connections may be consuming a disproportionate amount of your time and energy without providing much in return. While it's essential to maintain a diverse network, consider trimming away connections that no longer serve your goals. It's not about being ruthless but about creating space for meaningful interactions.

Leveraging Relationships for Opportunities

Now that you've identified your key connections, it's time to leverage these relationships for opportunities. The 20% of your network can introduce you to potential employers, collaborators, mentors, or investors who can help you advance in your career or personal endeavors.

One of the most effective ways to do this is through the principle of reciprocity. When you genuinely help others, they are more inclined to help you in return. By being a resource for your network, you not only strengthen your relationships but also position yourself as a valuable asset. Whether it's sharing your expertise, making introductions, or simply offering a listening ear, your generosity will be appreciated and reciprocated.

Additionally, focus on strategic networking events and activities. Rather than spreading yourself thin, invest your time and effort in events and gatherings where you are most likely to meet individuals who align with your goals. Be sure to follow up after these encounters, showing your appreciation and expressing your desire to continue the conversation.

Maintaining Meaningful Connections

In the fast-paced world we live in, maintaining meaningful connections can be a challenge. However, it's vital for long-term success. To achieve this, consider implementing the Pareto principle in your approach.

First, prioritize quality over quantity. Rather than aiming for a vast number of shallow connections, invest in fewer, deeper relationships. These are the connections that will stand the test of time and continue to provide value throughout your life.

Next, stay organized. Use tools like CRM (Customer Relationship Management) software to keep track of your interactions and important details about your connections. Set reminders to reach out, not just when you need something, but to nurture the relationship genuinely.

Furthermore, make an effort to meet face-to-face whenever possible. While digital communication has its benefits, there's no substitute for a personal connection. Share meals, attend conferences, or simply catch up over a coffee. These moments can solidify relationships in a way that emails and text messages cannot.

Finally, express gratitude. A heartfelt thank you can go a long way in strengthening a relationship. Take the time to acknowledge the support and opportunities your connections have provided. People appreciate knowing that their efforts are recognized and valued.

Networking is a powerful tool for personal and professional growth. By applying the Pareto principle, you can optimize your networking efforts, building a valuable network that opens doors to opportunities and support. Remember to focus on building quality connections, leveraging relationships through reciprocity, and maintaining these relationships with care. Your network can be a source of inspiration, guidance, and endless possibilities on your journey to success and fulfillment.

8.3 Family and Pareto

In the intricate dance of modern life, one of the most delicate acts we must master is finding balance. Our careers, our ambitions, and our aspirations often consume our thoughts and energy. However, in the quest for success, it's all too easy to overlook the most precious facet of our lives—our families. In this sub-chapter, we'll delve into how the Pareto principle can help you strike a harmonious chord between your personal and professional life, streamline your parenting approach for maximum impact, and create unbreakable bonds within your family.

Balancing Work and Family Life

One of the most common challenges we face is the struggle to balance our demanding work commitments with our desire to be present for our families. It often feels like a juggling act, with one ball always in danger of dropping. The Pareto principle, surprisingly, can provide a solution to this perpetual dilemma.

1: Prioritizing Quality Time

Instead of attempting to divide your time equally between work and family, Pareto suggests focusing on the vital 20%

that truly matters. In this context, quality time with your family takes precedence over quantity. When you're with your loved ones, be fully present. Put away your devices, silence the incessant chatter of the outside world, and immerse yourself in the moment. These focused, quality interactions can create more profound connections than distracted, quantity-driven encounters.

2: Communication Strategies

Effective communication lies at the heart of maintaining a balance between work and family. By using Pareto thinking, you can identify the critical areas that require clear and honest communication. This may involve discussing your work schedule with your family, setting boundaries to protect your personal time, or involving your children in decisions that affect the family as a whole. Open dialogue can prevent misunderstandings and foster a supportive atmosphere at home.

3: Resolving Conflicts Efficiently

No family is immune to conflicts. They're a natural part of human relationships. However, the Pareto principle teaches us that most conflicts can be traced back to a handful of core issues. By identifying these root causes and addressing them directly, you can resolve conflicts more efficiently and prevent recurring arguments. Remember, it's not about avoiding conflicts altogether, but about managing them effectively.

Parenting with Efficiency

Parenting is a full-time job in itself. The demands of modern parenthood can be overwhelming, but applying the Pareto principle can help you navigate this challenging terrain more efficiently.

1: Pareto-Driven Parenting

In parenting, as in life, not all efforts yield the same results. The Pareto principle suggests that a minority of your actions as a parent will have a significant impact on your children's well-being. Identify these high-impact activities and focus your energy there. For instance, spending quality one-on-one time with each child, actively listening to their concerns, and providing them with opportunities for growth are all high-impact actions.

2: Time Management for Parents

As a parent, time is your most valuable resource, and it often seems in short supply. Applying Pareto principles to your daily routines can help you reclaim precious moments. Streamline household chores, delegate responsibilities within the family, and use technology to your advantage. The time you save can be reinvested in meaningful interactions with your children.

3: Teaching Life Skills

One of the most powerful gifts you can give your children
is the ability to navigate life's challenges effectively.
Pareto's efficiency mindset extends to parenting by
emphasizing the importance of teaching your children vital
life skills. Encourage independence, critical thinking, and
problem-solving abilities. By doing so, you empower them
to thrive in a complex world.

Strengthening Family Bonds
The heart of any family lies in the connections between its
members. Strong family bonds provide a source of love,
support, and resilience. The Pareto principle can guide you
in nurturing these precious relationships.

1: Building Traditions and Rituals

Family traditions and rituals create a sense of belonging
and identity. Pareto suggests that focusing on a few
meaningful traditions can be more impactful than trying to
maintain a multitude of them. Choose activities that
resonate with your family and instill a sense of
togetherness.

2: Quality Over Quantity

Much like in the balance between work and family life,
Pareto teaches us that the quality of time spent together
matters more than the quantity. Rather than trying to pack

your schedule with family outings, prioritize meaningful moments. A simple evening of storytelling or board games can be more cherished than a dozen rushed outings.

3: Celebrating Individuality

While family bonds are essential, it's also vital to recognize and celebrate the individuality of each family member. Pareto's principle of focusing on the vital few applies here too. Acknowledge and celebrate each family member's unique talents and achievements. Encourage open communication to understand their dreams and aspirations.

Remember that applying the Pareto principle to your family life doesn't mean simplifying your relationships to mere percentages. Instead, it's about optimizing your efforts to create more meaningful connections, efficient parenting, and stronger family bonds. By doing so, you can savor the richness of your family life while achieving your professional ambitions.

Chapter 9: Health and Fitness: Pareto-Style

9.1 Pareto in Fitness

In this sub-chapter, we embark on a journey to transform our fitness routines into efficient powerhouses of health and vitality. We'll dive into the Pareto principle's application in fitness, uncovering the secrets to maximizing your workout efficiency, understanding the crucial role of nutrition, and adopting sustainable healthy habits that will stand the test of time.

Maximizing Workout Efficiency

Your journey to health begins with understanding that not all workouts are created equal. The Pareto principle teaches us that 20% of our efforts yield 80% of the results. So, let's focus on those workouts that give you the most bang for your buck.

1: Efficient Workouts

Efficient workouts are the cornerstone of the Pareto approach to fitness. Instead of spending hours at the gym, focus on shorter, high-intensity workouts that target multiple muscle groups simultaneously. Activities like circuit training, HIIT (High-Intensity Interval Training), and compound exercises allow you to get more done in less time.

Consider this: a 30-minute HIIT session can burn as many calories as an hour-long steady-state cardio workout. It not only saves you time but also keeps your metabolism revved up for hours after you're done.

2: Goal-Oriented Training

Pareto in fitness isn't just about working hard; it's about working smart. Define clear fitness goals for yourself, whether it's building muscle, improving endurance, or losing weight. Tailor your workouts to align with these goals.

For instance, if your goal is muscle gain, focus on strength training exercises that target major muscle groups like squats, deadlifts, and bench presses. By honing in on these high-impact exercises, you can achieve substantial results with a shorter time investment.

3: Rest and Recovery

The Pareto principle extends to rest and recovery as well. In fitness, the 80/20 rule means that 80% of your progress occurs outside the gym. Adequate rest and recovery are vital for muscle repair and growth.

Ensure you're getting enough sleep and allowing your body to recuperate between intense workouts. Overtraining can lead to burnout and injury, which will set you back rather than propel you forward. By focusing on quality over quantity, you can make your workout time truly count.

Nutrition and Pareto

Now that we've optimized our workouts let's turn our attention to nutrition—the fuel that powers your fitness journey.

1: The 80/20 Plate

Pareto in nutrition is about making smart choices that yield significant results. Consider adopting the 80/20 plate philosophy, where 80% of your diet consists of nutrient-dense, whole foods like lean proteins, vegetables, fruits, and whole grains. The remaining 20% can be reserved for indulgences and treats.

This approach ensures you get the essential vitamins, minerals, and macronutrients your body needs for optimal performance while allowing for occasional indulgences to maintain a healthy relationship with food.

2: Meal Planning and Preparation

Meal planning and preparation are Pareto's allies in the kitchen. Spend some time each week planning your meals and snacks. Preparing nutritious meals in advance saves time, reduces the temptation of unhealthy choices, and helps you stick to your dietary goals.

Consider batch-cooking staples like grains, lean proteins, and vegetables. Having these readily available will make it easier to assemble balanced meals, especially during busy days.

3: Hydration and Recovery

Don't underestimate the power of hydration and post-workout recovery. Proper hydration is essential for overall health and can impact exercise performance. Aim to drink enough water throughout the day, and consider replenishing electrolytes during intense workouts.

Additionally, recovery meals or snacks with a balanced ratio of protein and carbohydrates are crucial to aid muscle repair and replenish glycogen stores after exercise.

Sustainable Healthy Habits
The Pareto principle isn't just about quick fixes; it's about building sustainable habits that will keep you on the path to wellness for the long haul.

1: Consistency Over Perfection

Consistency is key. Instead of striving for perfection, aim for steady progress. Small, consistent changes to your diet and exercise routine are more likely to become lasting habits than drastic overhauls that are difficult to maintain.

2: Mindful Eating

Practice mindful eating. Pay attention to your body's hunger and fullness cues. Eating slowly and savoring your food can help prevent overeating and promote a healthy relationship with food.

3: Setting Realistic Goals

Set achievable fitness and nutrition goals. Unrealistic expectations can lead to frustration and disappointment. Celebrate your successes, no matter how small, and use them as motivation to keep going.

Embracing the Pareto principle in fitness involves optimizing your workouts for efficiency, making informed nutrition choices, and developing sustainable healthy habits. Remember, it's not about working harder but working smarter. By applying these principles, you'll be well on your way to achieving your fitness goals and enjoying a healthier, happier life.

9.2 Mental Health and Well-being

In the grand scheme of our lives, we often find ourselves engaged in a relentless pursuit of success and achievement. We chase our dreams, climb ladders, and strive for excellence. Yet, in this whirlwind, it's easy to overlook one of the most vital aspects of our existence—our mental health and overall well-being.

It's no secret that our mental health plays a pivotal role in our ability to lead fulfilling lives. Just as the Pareto principle teaches us to focus on the vital few, it applies beautifully to the realm of mental health and well-being, allowing us to cultivate a state of inner balance and harmony.

Stress Management with Pareto

Let's start our journey within by addressing a universal adversary—stress. Stress can often feel like an insurmountable mountain, but with the Pareto principle as your guiding light, you can begin to break it down into manageable parts.

1: Identifying Stress Triggers

Stress, in its various forms, can stem from a multitude of sources—work pressures, financial worries, relationship strains, or even personal expectations. The first step in managing stress with Pareto is identifying its triggers.

Take a moment to reflect on what situations or circumstances tend to induce stress in your life. Perhaps it's tight deadlines at work, or maybe it's the constant influx of information from your digital devices. By pinpointing these triggers, you empower yourself to address them more effectively.

2: Pareto Solutions for Stress

Now that you've identified the stressors in your life, it's time to apply the Pareto principle to find efficient solutions.

Consider the 80/20 rule: often, a small portion of your stressors contributes to the majority of your overall stress.

For instance, 20% of your tasks at work may cause 80% of your stress. Identify these high-impact stressors and devise strategies to address them directly.

Delegate tasks, set boundaries, and learn to say no when necessary. The Pareto approach encourages you to channel your energy and resources where they will have the most significant impact on reducing stress.

3: Relaxation and Mindfulness Techniques

Stress management isn't solely about tackling stressors head-on. It's equally essential to cultivate practices that promote relaxation and mental well-being.

Mindfulness meditation, for instance, is a practice that aligns seamlessly with Pareto principles. It encourages you to focus your attention on the present moment—the vital few—rather than being scattered across countless distractions. By practicing mindfulness, you can learn to let go of unnecessary mental clutter and find tranquility in simplicity.

Additionally, consider the 80/20 approach to relaxation activities. Identify the small percentage of activities that bring you the most profound sense of peace and relaxation. It could be reading a book, taking a walk in nature, or spending quality time with loved ones. Prioritize these activities to maximize their impact on your mental well-being.

Prioritizing Mental Health

Mental health isn't just the absence of stress; it's a holistic state of well-being that encompasses emotional, psychological, and social dimensions. Just as you prioritize your tasks using the Pareto principle, you must also prioritize your mental health.

1: Conscious Spending and Pareto

Imagine your mental health as an investment portfolio. You want to allocate your mental resources wisely to achieve optimal returns in the form of emotional resilience and psychological well-being.

Conscious spending in this context means being mindful of where you allocate your mental resources. Just as you wouldn't squander your financial assets on frivolous expenses, don't squander your mental energy on unproductive thoughts and worries.

Identify the mental activities that truly nourish your well-being—self-reflection, positive affirmations, or seeking professional guidance when needed—and allocate your mental energy accordingly. This is a Pareto-driven approach to mental health, where you focus on the vital few activities that yield the most significant returns in terms of well-being.

2: Sustainable Choices

Pareto principles extend beyond time management; they also apply to lifestyle choices. Just as you aim to streamline your daily tasks, consider streamlining your lifestyle choices to prioritize mental health.

Evaluate your daily routines and habits. Are there activities or behaviors that drain your mental energy without offering substantial benefits? It might be excessive screen time, unhealthy eating habits, or lack of physical activity. Identify these low-impact choices and gradually replace them with healthier alternatives.

Remember, the Pareto approach to mental health encourages you to focus on the critical 20% of choices that contribute to 80% of your well-being. This might involve making smarter dietary choices, practicing regular exercise, or incorporating mindfulness into your daily routine.

3: Nurturing a Gratitude-Driven Lifestyle

Gratitude is a powerful tool in your journey to prioritize mental health. By adopting an attitude of gratitude, you shift your focus from what you lack to what you already have—a fundamental aspect of Pareto principles.

Start each day by acknowledging the positive aspects of your life. It could be the warmth of the sun on your skin, the support of loved ones, or the opportunities that lie ahead. This simple practice redirects your mental energy towards the vital few elements that bring joy and contentment.

Moreover, expressing gratitude to others not only strengthens your relationships but also fosters a sense of connection and emotional well-being. It's a prime example of how Pareto principles can enhance your mental health by focusing on the essential aspects that contribute to a fulfilling life.

Mindfulness and Efficiency

The Pareto principle, which suggests that 20% of your efforts yield 80% of the results, can be applied to your mindfulness practice. By focusing on the essential aspects of mindfulness—such as deep presence and intentional awareness—you can unlock the majority of its benefits.

Imagine the impact of dedicating just 20% of your day to mindfulness practices. This intentional investment can lead to an 80% increase in focus, productivity, and overall well-being. In this sense, mindfulness becomes a powerful catalyst for efficiency, allowing you to accomplish more while experiencing greater satisfaction in your pursuits.

Practical ways to incorporate mindfulness into your daily life:

Mindful Task Execution: When performing tasks, whether mundane or complex, immerse yourself fully in the activity. Pay attention to the details, the sensations, and the emotions that arise. By embracing each task with mindfulness, you infuse it with purpose and efficiency.

Mindful Technology Use: Technology, while powerful, can be a double-edged sword when it comes to efficiency. Mindfully manage your tech use by setting boundaries.

Designate specific times for checking emails and social media, and avoid mindless scrolling.

Mindful Communication: Prioritize active listening in your interactions with others. Truly engage with what they are saying, without formulating your response in advance. This mindful approach to communication fosters deeper connections and resolves conflicts more effectively.

In the realm of mental health and well-being, the Pareto principle acts as a compass, guiding you toward efficient stress management, mindful prioritization, and the cultivation of a grateful, resilient mind. Remember, your mental health is a precious asset, and by applying Pareto principles, you can make the most of it.

Now, as we delve deeper into the realm of well-being, let's shift our focus to an essential facet—physical health. In the next section, we'll explore how Pareto principles can help you achieve a balanced, healthy lifestyle that aligns with your goals and aspirations.

9.3 Sleep and Recovery

In this fast-paced world where it often feels like every minute counts, it's easy to underestimate the profound impact that sleep and recovery can have on our lives. The truth is, sleep isn't a luxury; it's a necessity. And when we apply the Pareto principle to our sleep patterns, we can unlock a wealth of benefits that ripple through every aspect of our lives.

Optimizing Sleep Patterns

Sleep is a foundational pillar of our overall well-being. Yet, many of us treat it as negotiable, often sacrificing it in pursuit of productivity or entertainment. The irony is that optimizing your sleep patterns can actually enhance your productivity, creativity, and overall health.

Imagine sleep as the charging station for your body and mind. To optimize your sleep patterns, consider the following key points:

- Consistency is Key: Your body loves routines. Try to go to bed and wake up at the same times every day, even on weekends. This consistency helps regulate your internal body clock.

- Create a Sleep-Inducing Environment: Make your bedroom a sanctuary for sleep. Ensure your room is dark, quiet, and cool. Invest in a comfortable mattress and pillows. Remove electronic devices that emit blue light, as it can interfere with your sleep-inducing hormone, melatonin.

- Limit Caffeine and Alcohol: Be mindful of your caffeine intake, especially in the afternoon and evening. Similarly, while alcohol may make you drowsy initially, it can disrupt your sleep patterns later in the night.

- Power Down Before Bed: Engaging in relaxing activities before bedtime can signal to your body that it's time to wind down. Consider reading a book, practicing meditation, or taking a warm bath.

- Watch Your Diet: Eating heavy meals or spicy foods close to bedtime can lead to discomfort and indigestion. Aim to finish eating at least two to three hours before sleep.

- Exercise Regularly: Regular physical activity can promote better sleep. However, try to complete your workouts a few hours before bedtime, as exercising too close to sleep can have the opposite effect.

- Manage Stress: High levels of stress and anxiety can wreak havoc on your sleep patterns. Practice stress-reduction techniques, such as deep breathing or mindfulness, to calm your mind before bedtime.

By applying the Pareto principle to your sleep patterns, you can identify the 20% of habits that contribute to 80% of your restorative sleep. These small but powerful changes can transform your nights and, consequently, your days.

Rest and Productivity
Once you've optimized your sleep patterns, you'll discover that the quality of your rest significantly impacts your productivity. When you wake up feeling refreshed and rejuvenated, you're better equipped to tackle the day's challenges with vigor and focus.

Here's the Pareto approach to ensuring your rest enhances your productivity:

- Short Naps for Quick Recharge: A short power nap of around 20 minutes can provide an instant boost in alertness and productivity. It's like hitting the reset button for your brain.

- Prioritize Deep Sleep: The most restorative sleep occurs during the deep, slow-wave stages of the sleep cycle. Aim to get more of this type of sleep by creating a comfortable sleep environment and adhering to a consistent sleep schedule.

- Beware of Over-Sleeping: While too little sleep is detrimental, oversleeping can also leave you feeling groggy. Try to limit your sleep to 7-9 hours per night, depending on your individual needs.

- Catnaps for Creativity: If you're looking to boost your creativity, consider the power of catnaps, which typically last between 10-20 minutes. They can provide a mental reset and foster innovative thinking.

- Quality Over Quantity: It's not just about the number of hours you sleep; it's about the quality of those hours. Focus on improving the depth and restorative aspects of your sleep rather than just extending your time in bed.

- Establish a Wind-Down Routine: As part of your Pareto-driven sleep strategy, create a calming bedtime routine that signals to your body that it's time to rest. This routine might include gentle stretches, journaling, or listening to soothing music.

The Power of Restorative Sleep

Now, let's delve into the incredible power of restorative sleep. Beyond merely feeling rested, it plays a pivotal role in your overall health and well-being. When you optimize your sleep patterns and prioritize rest, you'll unlock a cascade of benefits that extend to every facet of your life.

1. Enhanced Cognitive Function: Adequate sleep sharpens your cognitive abilities. It improves your memory, problem-solving skills, and decision-making capabilities. In essence, sleep is like a cognitive enhancer, allowing you to tackle challenges with greater clarity.

2. Emotional Resilience: Restorative sleep bolsters your emotional well-being. It helps regulate mood, reduces irritability, and enhances your ability to handle stress. You'll find yourself more patient and better equipped to navigate life's ups and downs.

3. Physical Health: The Pareto principle also applies to your physical health. Quality sleep promotes better immune function, reducing your susceptibility to illness. It aids in weight management by regulating hunger hormones, and it supports cardiovascular health.

4. Energy and Vitality: With sufficient restorative sleep, you'll wake up each morning with a surge of energy. You'll find yourself more motivated to pursue your goals and engage in physical activities. The 20% of sleep practices that yield 80% of the energy become evident.

5. Longevity: Numerous studies have linked optimal sleep patterns with increased lifespan. It's not just about living

longer; it's about living better and enjoying a higher quality of life in your later years.

6. Creativity and Innovation: Creativity flourishes in well-rested minds. A good night's sleep can be the breeding ground for innovative ideas, as it allows your brain to consolidate memories and make unique connections.

7. Stress Reduction: The power of restorative sleep in managing stress cannot be overstated. It provides your body with the opportunity to repair and rejuvenate, reducing the physical toll of stress on your body.

8. Relationships and Communication: When you're well-rested, you're better equipped to engage in meaningful conversations and empathize with others. Your relationships will benefit from your newfound patience and emotional stability.

In the grand scheme of your life's journey, optimizing your sleep patterns and embracing the power of restorative sleep may seem like a small piece of the puzzle, but it's one that holds the potential to transform the entire picture. It's a Pareto principle in action – the 20% effort that yields 80% of the rewards.

So, my dear readers, as you embark on this journey to unlock the potential of restorative sleep, remember that it's not just about getting more sleep; it's about getting the right kind of sleep – the sleep that rejuvenates your mind, body, and spirit. Embrace the Pareto approach to sleep, and you'll awaken each day ready to conquer the world with renewed vigor and zest for life. Sweet dreams!

Chapter 10: Creativity and Pareto: Doing More with Less

10.1 Creative Efficiency

Creativity is the lifeblood of innovation and progress. It's the spark that ignites our imagination, drives our passion, and fuels our dreams. Yet, often, we find ourselves grappling with creative blocks, struggling to make the most of our creative potential. In this sub-chapter, we'll explore how the Pareto principle can revolutionize the way we approach creativity.

Pareto in Creative Processes

Imagine a world where your creative endeavors are not bound by time-consuming, inefficient processes. A world where you can harness the power of the Pareto principle to do more with less, leaving you with more time and energy to focus on what truly matters – your creative output.

The Pareto principle can be a game-changer in creative processes. It encourages us to identify the vital few elements that contribute the most to our creative endeavors. By recognizing the 20% of factors that yield 80% of our creative output, we can streamline our creative processes and eliminate the noise that hinders our progress.

1: Identifying the Vital Few

Start by examining your creative process. What are the essential elements that consistently lead to your best work? It might be the initial brainstorming sessions, the moments of solitude, or the collaborative exchanges with peers. These are the vital few aspects that deserve your attention and focus.

Take a closer look at your past creative projects. Identify the common denominators that contributed significantly to their success. Was it the research phase, the hours of practice, or a specific routine that put you in the creative zone? By recognizing these patterns, you can channel your efforts more effectively.

2: Streamlining Your Creative Workflow

Once you've pinpointed the vital few, it's time to streamline your creative workflow. Pareto reminds us that not all creative activities are created equal. Instead of spending equal time and energy on every aspect of your project, allocate your resources wisely.

For instance, if you discover that the ideation phase is where your most innovative ideas flourish, devote more time to brainstorming and idea generation. Trim down the less impactful activities that don't contribute significantly to your creative output.

3: Eliminating Time-Wasters

Creative processes are notorious for their time-wasting elements. Endless revisions, procrastination, and perfectionism can eat away at your productive hours.

Pareto invites you to identify and eliminate these creative time-wasters.

Consider setting strict time limits for specific creative tasks. Embrace the concept of "good enough" rather than endlessly pursuing perfection. By doing so, you free up time and mental space to channel your creative energy where it truly matters.

Eliminating Creative Blocks
Creative blocks are the bane of every artist, writer, musician, and innovator. They can strike unexpectedly, leaving us frustrated and drained. Fortunately, Pareto offers a fresh perspective on overcoming these blocks and reigniting our creative spark.

1: Breaking Down the Creative Wall

When faced with a creative block, our instinct is often to push harder, work longer, or force inspiration. However, Pareto encourages us to take a step back and analyze the situation. What is the root cause of this blockage?

By identifying the specific challenges that hinder your creative flow, you can tackle them more effectively. Perhaps it's self-doubt, fear of failure, or external distractions. Once you've isolated the problem, you can develop targeted strategies to address it.

2: The Power of Rest and Play

Creativity thrives in a relaxed and playful environment. Pareto reminds us that it's not about the quantity of work but the quality of our efforts. Taking regular breaks, engaging in activities that refresh your mind, and allowing your subconscious to process ideas can be the keys to unlocking creativity.

Consider adopting techniques like the Pomodoro method, which breaks work into focused intervals followed by short breaks. During these breaks, engage in activities that relax and recharge you. It could be a short walk, a quick meditation session, or even a few minutes of light reading. These pauses can provide the mental reset you need to overcome creative blocks.

3: Embracing Constraints

Creativity often flourishes within constraints. It forces us to think outside the box, find innovative solutions, and make the most of limited resources. Pareto encourages us to embrace constraints as opportunities rather than limitations.

When faced with creative challenges, set clear boundaries. Whether it's a word limit for your writing, a tight budget for your project, or a specific theme for your art, constraints can serve as catalysts for ingenuity. They push you to explore unconventional paths and tap into your creativity more deeply.

Nurturing Creative Inspiration

The essence of creativity lies in inspiration – those moments when ideas flow effortlessly, and you feel in perfect harmony with your creative self. Pareto's principles can help you nurture and sustain these bursts of inspiration.

1: Cultivating a Creative Environment

Your physical and mental surroundings play a significant role in sparking inspiration. Pareto suggests that by decluttering your workspace, organizing your thoughts, and creating a conducive environment for creativity, you can invite inspiration more readily.

Consider dedicating a specific space for your creative pursuits, free from distractions. Surround yourself with objects, colors, and stimuli that resonate with your creative spirit. By curating your environment, you can create a sanctuary for inspiration to flourish.

2: Curiosity and Diverse Experiences

Inspiration often emerges from diverse experiences and curiosity about the world around us. Pareto encourages us to explore various interests and engage in activities that broaden our horizons.

Feed your curiosity by reading widely, trying new hobbies, and immersing yourself in different cultures. These experiences enrich your creative reservoir, providing a vast pool of ideas and perspectives to draw upon when inspiration strikes.

3: Reflect and Capture Insights

Inspiration can be fleeting, like a passing breeze. To make the most of it, Pareto suggests keeping a creative journal or recording your insights as they come. This practice ensures that you capture those precious moments of inspiration and can revisit them when needed.

Take the time to reflect on your creative journey regularly. Celebrate your breakthroughs, learn from your challenges, and document your ideas, no matter how small. Over time, you'll build a valuable resource of inspiration that can fuel your creativity in the future.

In the realm of creativity, Pareto's principles offer a refreshing perspective. They guide us to identify the core elements of our creative process, eliminate obstacles, and nurture inspiration. By applying these principles, you can unlock your full creative potential and embark on a journey of doing more with less – a journey that leads to greater innovation, satisfaction, and creative fulfillment.

10.2 Innovation and Pareto

Innovation—the word alone conjures visions of breakthrough ideas, game-changing inventions, and revolutionary advancements. It's the lifeblood of progress and the driving force behind the world's most successful individuals and organizations. But what if I told you that innovation, too, can be harnessed and optimized through the lens of the Pareto principle?

Identifying Innovative Ideas

Innovation often seems like a mystical realm, reserved for the Einsteins and Jobs of the world. We tend to think of it as a spark of genius, an elusive muse that occasionally graces us with its presence. However, when we apply the Pareto principle, we discover that innovation can be a systematic process rather than a random stroke of luck.

Unlocking the power of Pareto in innovation begins with a shift in perspective. Instead of waiting for that elusive "aha" moment, start by observing the world around you. Pay close attention to problems, inefficiencies, and unmet needs. These are your clues, your entry points into the realm of innovation.

For instance, let's take the story of James Dyson, the inventor of the bagless vacuum cleaner. Dyson didn't just stumble upon his revolutionary idea. He spent years studying the inefficiencies of traditional vacuum cleaners, observing how they lost suction power as they filled with dust. His "aha" moment came when he realized that a cyclonic separation system could maintain suction by separating dust from air.

This process of identifying innovative ideas is often about asking the right questions. What challenges frustrate you or those around you? What aspects of your life or work could be more efficient or enjoyable? The answers to these questions can be fertile ground for groundbreaking innovations.

Resource Allocation for Innovation
Once you've identified a potential innovation, the next step is to allocate resources strategically. This is where Pareto can be your guiding star. The essence of the Pareto principle is that 20% of your efforts lead to 80% of the results. Similarly, in innovation, focusing your resources on the most promising ideas can yield extraordinary outcomes.

Consider the story of Google's "20% time" policy, which allowed employees to spend a fifth of their workweek on side projects of their choice. This policy gave birth to some of Google's most iconic products, including Gmail and Google News. By allocating a relatively small portion of their time to innovative pursuits, Google reaped an outsized harvest of groundbreaking ideas.

When applying the Pareto principle to resource allocation for innovation, start by prioritizing the most promising ideas from your pool of innovative concepts. Invest time, energy, and, if necessary, financial resources into these projects. Remember that not all ideas will yield equally impressive results, so it's crucial to be selective and focus on the innovations with the greatest potential impact.

Turning Ideas into Reality
Innovation isn't merely about generating ideas; it's about bringing those ideas to life. This phase can be particularly

challenging because it requires a blend of creativity, strategic thinking, and execution. But fear not, for the Pareto principle can illuminate the path ahead.

Let's delve into the story of Airbnb. The concept of renting out a spare room to strangers was initially met with skepticism. Yet, the founders, Brian Chesky, Joe Gebbia, and Nathan Blecharczyk, didn't let this deter them. They turned to the Pareto principle to focus on the most critical aspect of their idea: the user experience.

By allocating their resources to creating high-quality photos and ensuring a seamless booking process, they transformed their innovative concept into a thriving global platform. They understood that the success of their innovation depended on the crucial 20% that would deliver 80% of the value to their users.

To turn your ideas into reality, start by breaking down the innovation process into manageable steps. Identify the key components that will have the most significant impact on the idea's success. This might involve refining the user experience, optimizing your product's features, or designing a compelling marketing strategy.

Next, allocate your resources and efforts accordingly. Remember, not all steps are created equal. The Pareto principle encourages you to focus on the vital few rather than the trivial many. By directing your energy toward the aspects that matter most, you can bring your innovative ideas to fruition more efficiently and effectively.

The marriage of innovation and the Pareto principle is a powerful one. It dispels the myth that innovation is solely the domain of geniuses and reveals it as a systematic process accessible to all. By identifying innovative ideas, allocating resources strategically, and turning those ideas into reality, you can harness the full potential of innovation while doing more with less. Your journey to becoming an innovation maven begins with a shift in perspective and a commitment to focusing on what truly matters.

10.3 Artistic Expression with Pareto

In the world of creativity, where imagination knows no bounds, the Pareto principle may not seem like an obvious ally. After all, art is often associated with boundless expression and the freedom to let ideas flow without constraint. But what if I told you that the Pareto principle could be the key to unlocking your artistic potential and allowing you to do more with less? Let's dive into this intriguing concept and discover how it can enhance your artistic pursuits.

Efficiency in Artistic Pursuits

Artists, whether they wield a brush, a camera, or any other tool of their trade, are no strangers to the creative process. It's a journey filled with inspiration, experimentation, and at times, frustration. But what if you could make this journey more efficient without stifling your creativity? Enter the Pareto principle.

At its core, the Pareto principle suggests that 80% of results come from 20% of efforts. How does this apply to art? Consider your creative process. In those moments of artistic brilliance, where your ideas flow effortlessly, you're likely in the 20% zone—the sweet spot of productivity. The key is to recognize these moments, harness them, and make them a central part of your creative routine.

1: Identifying Your Creative Zone

Start by reflecting on your past creative endeavors. When did you produce your best work? What circumstances and environments led to those moments of artistic brilliance? These questions can help you pinpoint when you're in your creative zone.

Once you've identified your creative zone, strive to replicate it. Create a workspace that resonates with your muse, whether it's a quiet room with soft lighting or a bustling café with ambient noise. The goal is to set the stage for those magical moments to occur more frequently.

2: Pareto-Driven Project Selection

Not every artistic project is created equal. Some will resonate more with your audience, while others might fall flat. Applying the Pareto principle to your artistic pursuits means being discerning about the projects you undertake.

Focus on the 20% of projects that have the potential to yield 80% of the results.

Consider your audience's preferences and your own passions. What type of art aligns with both? By selecting projects that strike a balance between your artistic passion and your audience's interests, you're more likely to achieve success without spreading yourself too thin.

Balancing Creativity and Practicality
Artists often grapple with the balance between creative freedom and practicality. The fear of sacrificing one's artistic vision for the sake of practicality can be a daunting hurdle. However, the Pareto principle can help you find equilibrium between these seemingly opposing forces.

1: Pareto-Driven Constraints

Constraints can be surprisingly liberating for artists. When you limit your choices, you're forced to think more creatively. Pareto suggests focusing on the essential 20% of elements that will yield 80% of the impact in your art. This might mean working with a limited color palette, restricting yourself to a specific style, or even embracing imperfections in your work.

Constraints encourage innovation and can lead to breakthroughs in your art. The key is to view constraints not as limitations but as opportunities to explore new facets of your creativity.

2: The Art of Editing

Editing is an essential part of the creative process, and the Pareto principle can guide your editing decisions. When you've completed a piece of art, step back and assess it objectively. What elements contribute the most to the piece's impact, emotion, or message? These are your vital 20%.

Focus on enhancing and refining these crucial elements while letting go of the extraneous 80%. Often, less is more in art, and by embracing the Pareto principle in your editing process, you can create more impactful and resonant pieces.

Sharing Your Art with the World
As an artist, you pour your heart and soul into your work, and sharing it with the world is a deeply personal and sometimes intimidating endeavor. But here's where the Pareto principle can truly shine, guiding you in efficiently getting your art out into the world.

1: Targeted Promotion

Rather than trying to promote your art to everyone, focus on the 20% of your audience that is most likely to connect with your work. Identify your niche—the group of people who share a genuine interest in your artistic style or subject matter. Tailor your promotional efforts to reach this audience effectively.

Utilize social media, art galleries, online platforms, or local exhibitions to connect with your niche audience. Engaging with the right audience not only saves time and effort but also leads to more meaningful interactions and opportunities for collaboration.

2: Collaboration and Networking

In the creative world, collaborations can be a powerful tool for expanding your reach and influence. Identify fellow artists or creative individuals who complement your work or share a similar artistic vision. By teaming up, you can leverage each other's strengths, resources, and audiences, achieving more together than you could alone.

Networking is also a vital aspect of promoting your art efficiently. Attend art events, workshops, and gatherings to connect with fellow artists and potential patrons. Building a supportive artistic community can help you navigate the complex landscape of the art world more effectively.

3: Leveraging Technology

In today's digital age, technology offers countless opportunities for artists to share their work with a global audience. Create a digital portfolio, maintain an engaging online presence, and explore platforms such as Instagram, Etsy, or Behance to showcase your art to a broader audience.

Additionally, consider using digital tools for marketing, tracking your audience's preferences, and streamlining administrative tasks. Technology can be a valuable ally in your efforts to efficiently share your art with the world.

The Pareto principle is not a restrictive framework for artists but a guiding principle that can enhance your creative journey. By identifying your creative zone, selecting projects strategically, embracing constraints, and focusing on what truly matters in your art, you can achieve more with less effort. Balancing creativity and practicality, and efficiently sharing your art with the world, are essential steps on your path to artistic success. Embrace the power of Pareto and watch your artistic endeavors flourish.

Chapter 11: Pareto in Education and Learning

11.1 Learning Effectively

In this subchapter, we're about to embark on a transformative journey—a journey that will unlock the secrets of efficient learning, unleashing your untapped potential. Learning effectively is not just about spending countless hours buried in textbooks or online courses; it's about working smarter, not harder. It's about applying the Pareto principle to your educational endeavors, ensuring that 20% of your efforts yield 80% of the results.

Pareto in Learning Efficiency

Imagine a world where you can master new skills, absorb knowledge like a sponge, and retain information effortlessly. Well, it's not a distant dream; it's a reality within your grasp. By understanding and harnessing the power of the Pareto principle, you can make the process of learning more efficient and enjoyable.

At its core, the Pareto principle in learning suggests that a small fraction of the material you encounter will provide the majority of your understanding and retention. The key to success lies in identifying this critical 20% and focusing your efforts there.

1: Identifying the Vital 20%

Imagine you're learning a new language. Instead of memorizing every word in the dictionary, start by learning the most common words and phrases. These constitute the vital 20% that will allow you to communicate effectively in most situations. Similarly, in any subject, there are fundamental concepts and key principles that form the foundation. Identify these, and you'll have a solid base on which to build your knowledge.

2: Quality over Quantity

It's a common misconception that spending more time studying equates to better learning. However, the Pareto principle tells us that it's the quality of your study time that matters most. Instead of mindlessly rereading your notes or textbooks, focus on active learning techniques. Engage with the material through summarization, self-testing, and explaining concepts to others. This not only reinforces your understanding but also ensures that you're dedicating your time to the most critical information.

3: Consistency is Key

Efficiency in learning also hinges on consistency. Regular, shorter study sessions are more effective than cramming. Spacing out your learning over time, known as spaced repetition, helps solidify your memory and comprehension. It's like building a sturdy bridge—one brick at a time— rather than trying to construct it all at once.

Study Techniques for Success

Now that we've explored the foundational principles of efficient learning, let's delve into specific study techniques that will propel you toward academic excellence. These techniques align with the Pareto principle, ensuring that you invest your time and energy where they'll yield the most significant results.

1: The Pomodoro Technique

Named after the Italian word for "tomato," this technique emphasizes short, focused bursts of studying followed by brief breaks. For example, study intensely for 25 minutes, then take a 5-minute break. This approach not only maximizes your concentration during study sessions but also prevents burnout and mental fatigue.

2: The Feynman Technique

Physicist Richard Feynman believed that if you couldn't explain a concept in simple terms, you didn't truly understand it. Apply this technique by picking a topic you're studying and explaining it as if you were teaching it to someone else. Identify gaps in your knowledge and revisit those areas for deeper understanding.

3: Mind Mapping

Mind mapping is a visual technique that helps you organize information and see connections between ideas. Start with a central concept and branch out into subtopics, using keywords and diagrams. This method engages both the left and right hemispheres of your brain, enhancing comprehension and memory.

Lifelong Learning and Growth

Learning doesn't stop when you graduate or complete a course. Lifelong learning is a commitment to continuous personal and professional growth. By embracing the Pareto principle in lifelong learning, you can ensure that your efforts yield ongoing benefits and opportunities.

1: Curiosity as a Driving Force

The great Albert Einstein once said, "I have no special talents. I am only passionately curious." Cultivate your curiosity—it's the engine that drives lifelong learning. Explore new subjects, ask questions, and seek answers. When you're genuinely interested in a topic, learning becomes a joyful pursuit rather than a chore.

2: Setting Clear Learning Goals

Incorporate SMART (Specific, Measurable, Achievable, Relevant, Time-bound) goals into your lifelong learning journey. Define what you want to achieve, how you'll measure progress, and the timeline for accomplishing each goal. This strategic approach ensures that your learning efforts align with your aspirations.

3: Expanding Horizons

Lifelong learning extends beyond traditional classrooms. Embrace a diverse range of learning experiences, from online courses and workshops to reading books and attending seminars. Connect with people who share your interests and engage in discussions to gain fresh perspectives. Remember that every encounter and experience contributes to your personal growth.

Remember that knowledge is the key to unlocking doors of opportunity. By applying the Pareto principle to your educational journey, you'll not only excel in your academic pursuits but also embark on a lifelong adventure of growth, exploration, and discovery. The path to becoming the best version of yourself starts with the choices you make today, so choose wisely and embrace the joy of learning.

11.2 Teaching and Education

In this subchapter, we delve into the exciting world of teaching and education, exploring how the Pareto principle can transform the way we learn and impart knowledge. It's not just about being a better student; it's about becoming a more effective teacher and making a lasting educational impact. So, let's embark on this journey to unlock the secrets of Pareto in the realm of education.

Applying Pareto in Teaching

Teaching is both an art and a science, a delicate dance between the instructor and the learner. And just like any other field, teaching can benefit immensely from the application of the Pareto principle.

1: Identifying Core Concepts

Imagine a classroom filled with eager minds, each with their unique abilities and interests. As a teacher, your challenge is to ensure that every student grasps the essential concepts that will serve as the foundation for more advanced knowledge. This is where Pareto comes into play.

Identify the 20% of topics or concepts that form the crux of your subject matter. These are the ideas that, when mastered, enable students to navigate through the rest of the material more effectively. Focus your teaching efforts on making these core concepts crystal clear. Explain them from various angles, provide real-world examples, and encourage questions to ensure complete comprehension.

2: Tailoring Your Teaching Methods

Not all students learn the same way. Some thrive on visual aids, others on hands-on activities, and some through verbal explanations. The Pareto principle encourages you to adapt your teaching methods to cater to the diversity of learning styles.

Identify the 20% of teaching methods that yield 80% of the results. These might include interactive discussions, problem-solving activities, or multimedia presentations. By incorporating a mix of these effective methods into your teaching approach, you create a more engaging and inclusive learning environment.

3: Maximizing Student Engagement

Engagement is the secret sauce of effective teaching. When students are actively involved in the learning process, they not only understand the material better but also retain it for longer periods.

Pareto suggests that you focus your attention on the 20% of activities or assignments that generate 80% of the student engagement. These could be group projects, debates, or hands-on experiments. The goal is to make learning an enjoyable and participatory experience, where students take ownership of their education.

Student-Centered Learning
Now, let's shift our focus to the heart of the educational experience: the students themselves. Student-centered learning is a revolutionary approach that places learners at the forefront of their educational journey.

1: Empowering Students

In a student-centered classroom, the teacher becomes a guide and facilitator rather than a sole source of knowledge.

The Pareto principle encourages you to empower students by letting them take the reins of their education.

Identify the 20% of responsibilities or decisions that students can make to drive 80% of their learning progress. Encourage them to set personal goals, choose projects that align with their interests, and take responsibility for their learning pace. When students have a say in their education, their motivation soars.

2: Customized Learning Paths

Every student is unique, with their strengths, weaknesses, and preferred learning styles. Pareto suggests that you focus on the 20% of individualized strategies that will lead to 80% of students reaching their full potential.

Offer personalized learning paths that cater to each student's needs. This might involve extra resources for struggling students, advanced materials for those who excel, or alternative assessments for diverse learners. Tailoring your approach ensures that no one is left behind.

3: Feedback and Reflection

Feedback is the compass that guides learning. The Pareto principle encourages you to invest your time in the 20% of feedback methods that will result in 80% of student improvement.

Provide timely and constructive feedback that highlights areas for growth while acknowledging achievements. Encourage students to reflect on their progress and set new goals. By fostering a culture of feedback and reflection, you enable continuous learning and improvement.

Educational Impact with Efficiency

The true measure of successful teaching lies not only in imparting knowledge but in making a lasting impact on students' lives. Pareto principles can help you achieve this by maximizing your educational efficiency.

1: Measuring Learning Outcomes

Identify the 20% of assessment methods or metrics that gauge 80% of student learning outcomes. These could include standardized tests, project evaluations, or peer reviews. Use these tools strategically to track and improve your teaching effectiveness.

2: Building Critical Thinking Skills

Critical thinking is the cornerstone of lifelong learning. Pareto encourages you to dedicate your efforts to the 20% of activities that foster 80% of critical thinking skills in students.

Encourage open-ended discussions, debates, and problem-solving exercises that challenge students to think deeply and critically. Equip them with the ability to analyze information, make informed decisions, and apply their knowledge beyond the classroom.

3: Inspiring a Love for Learning

Ultimately, the goal of education is to ignite a lifelong passion for learning. Identify the 20% of inspirational moments or experiences that fuel 80% of students' curiosity and enthusiasm for learning.

Share captivating stories, real-world applications, and success stories from individuals who have applied their knowledge to make a difference. Show students that learning is not confined to textbooks but is a gateway to endless possibilities.

As an educator, you have the power to transform lives through the Pareto principles. By focusing on the essentials, tailoring your approach, and maximizing efficiency, you can create a dynamic and student-centered learning environment that empowers students to thrive. Education becomes a journey of discovery, where both teachers and students embark on a path of continuous growth and fulfillment.

11.3 Specialized Knowledge and Expertise

In the ever-evolving landscape of knowledge and expertise, the Pareto principle is a guiding star, illuminating the path to mastery and relevance. In this subchapter, we'll embark on a transformative journey through the world of specialized knowledge, exploring how Pareto's wisdom can help you become an expert, master key skills, and stay relevant in a fast-paced world.

Becoming an Expert with Pareto

You've heard it said that it takes 10,000 hours to become an expert in a particular field. While this notion of deliberate practice holds some merit, the Pareto principle suggests a more nuanced approach. Instead of spreading your efforts thin across a broad range of topics, Pareto encourages you to focus on the vital few that truly matter.

1: Identify Your Vital Few

To become an expert, you must first identify the core principles, concepts, or skills within your chosen field that will yield the most significant results. These are your "vital few." Imagine them as the foundation of a grand edifice—a skyscraper of knowledge and expertise. Without a solid foundation, your pursuit of mastery may crumble.

Start by conducting a thorough assessment of your field. What are the key concepts that form the bedrock? What skills are in high demand? What trends are shaping the future? By identifying these critical elements, you can hone your focus and build your expertise more efficiently.

2: Deliberate Learning and Practice

Once you've pinpointed your vital few, it's time to immerse yourself in deliberate learning and practice. This isn't about mindlessly consuming information; it's about active engagement and purposeful application.

Break down your specialized knowledge into manageable chunks and tackle them systematically. Allocate your time and energy to these high-impact areas. Seek out the best resources, mentors, or courses that can accelerate your learning. Practice consistently, refining your skills, and pushing your boundaries.

Remember, expertise is a journey, not a destination. Along the way, you'll encounter challenges and setbacks, but perseverance and resilience are your allies on this quest.

3: The Feedback Loop of Improvement

One of the remarkable aspects of the Pareto principle is its emphasis on feedback and continuous improvement. As you accumulate knowledge and experience, it's essential to maintain a feedback loop. Seek out mentors, coaches, or peers who can provide constructive insights and help you refine your expertise.

Regularly assess your progress and adjust your learning strategies accordingly. Are you investing your time in the most impactful areas? Are there new developments in your field that demand your attention? Adaptation and flexibility are crucial components of expertise.

Mastering Key Skills

In the pursuit of expertise, mastering key skills is akin to honing the sharpest tools in your toolbox. Whether you're a musician, a scientist, an athlete, or an entrepreneur, your skills are your instruments of creation and impact.

1: The Power of Focus

Focus is the linchpin of skill mastery. While it may be tempting to dabble in various skills, Pareto's wisdom advises a different approach. Concentrate your efforts on a select few skills that align with your goals and passions.

Consider the 80/20 rule: 80% of your desired outcomes often result from 20% of your efforts. Identify the vital skills that will drive the majority of your success and pour your energy into them. Dedicate time each day or week for deliberate skill development, and watch your mastery grow.

2: Deliberate Skill Practice

Skill mastery doesn't happen overnight. It requires consistent, deliberate practice. This concept, often referred to as "the 10,000-hour rule," emphasizes that to become a true expert in a skill, you must put in deliberate, focused practice for a substantial amount of time.

But here's where Pareto's principle comes into play. While quantity matters, quality matters even more. It's not just about logging hours; it's about making those hours count. Break down your skill into its constituent parts, identify weaknesses, and target them with precision. Seek feedback and guidance from mentors or experts in your field to refine your practice.

3: Lifelong Skill Maintenance

Mastery is not a static state; it's a dynamic process. Once you've attained a high level of proficiency in a skill, the journey doesn't end. In a rapidly changing world, it's crucial to maintain and update your skills to stay relevant.

Stay attuned to emerging trends and technologies in your field. Continually seek opportunities for improvement and expansion. Remember that even the most seasoned experts must adapt to the evolving landscape.

Staying Relevant in a Fast-Paced World

In today's fast-paced world, the only constant is change. Staying relevant is not only about what you know but also about how you adapt and apply that knowledge. Pareto's wisdom can be your compass in navigating the ever-shifting currents of expertise and relevance.

1: Lifelong Learning Mindset

Embrace a lifelong learning mindset. Recognize that learning doesn't end with formal education or reaching a certain level of expertise. It's an ongoing process, and your willingness to learn new things keeps you agile and adaptable.

Stay curious and open to new ideas and perspectives. Seek out opportunities for learning, whether through books, courses, workshops, or mentorship. In a world where information is readily available, the true skill lies in discerning valuable knowledge from the noise.

2: Agility and Adaptation

The ability to adapt is a hallmark of relevance. As industries and technologies evolve, be willing to pivot and explore new avenues. Your existing expertise can be a strong foundation for branching into related fields or tackling emerging challenges.

Stay connected with your professional network, and actively participate in discussions and forums relevant to your expertise. Engage with peers and thought leaders to exchange ideas and insights. Collaboration and adaptation go hand in hand.

3: Innovation and Creativity

In a world driven by innovation, creativity is a powerful tool for staying relevant. The Pareto principle encourages you to focus your creative efforts on the areas that matter most—your vital few.

Think critically, challenge conventions, and seek innovative solutions within your domain. Explore interdisciplinary connections that can spark fresh ideas.

Remember that innovation often arises at the intersection of different fields, so don't be afraid to draw inspiration from diverse sources.

As you embark on your journey toward expertise and relevance, let Pareto's wisdom guide you. By identifying your vital few, practicing deliberately, mastering key skills, and maintaining a lifelong learning mindset, you'll not only become an expert but also remain a dynamic and influential force in our fast-paced world. Mastery is not an end; it's an ongoing adventure, and you are the author of your expertise.

Chapter 12: Problem-Solving and Decision Making with Pareto

12.1 Pareto-Driven Problem Solving

In the labyrinth of life, problems are the threads that weave a complex narrative. From the trivial daily conundrums to the monumental challenges that shape our destinies, problem-solving is a skill that can turn obstacles into stepping stones. In this chapter, we embark on a journey to master the art of Pareto-driven problem-solving, a powerful approach that enables us to focus on what truly matters, identify the core issues, analyze data efficiently, and implement effective solutions.

Identifying Core Issues

Imagine you're lost in a dense forest. You could wander aimlessly, exploring every nook and cranny, or you could pause, take a deep breath, and use your compass to find your way. In problem-solving, the Pareto principle is that compass—it directs your attention to the vital few among the trivial many.

Identifying core issues begins with a shift in perspective. Instead of being overwhelmed by the sheer volume of problems, you learn to ask the right questions. What are the underlying causes of this problem? What are the consequences of not addressing it? What is the impact of this issue on your life or organization?

1: The Power of Asking "Why"

One of the most effective tools in your problem-solving toolbox is the simple question, "Why?" By asking "Why" repeatedly, you peel back the layers of complexity to reveal the root cause of a problem. This technique, often referred to as the "Five Whys," was popularized by Toyota and has since been embraced by problem-solvers worldwide.

For example, let's say you're frequently running late for work. Asking "Why am I late?" might lead to answers like, "Because I overslept." But asking "Why did I oversleep?" could uncover deeper issues like poor sleep habits or an overloaded schedule. By digging deeper, you pinpoint the real problem and can take targeted action to address it.

2: Focus on High-Impact Problems

Pareto's wisdom encourages us to prioritize our efforts where they will make the most significant difference. Not all problems are created equal, and some have a more substantial impact on our lives or organizations than others. To identify the core issues, consider the 80/20 rule: Which 20% of the problems are causing 80% of the negative consequences?

For instance, in a business context, you might find that a small number of product defects are responsible for the majority of customer complaints. By allocating resources to address these specific defects, you can improve customer satisfaction dramatically and reduce the overall workload.

Data Analysis and Pareto

Once you've identified the core issues, the next step in Pareto-driven problem-solving is harnessing the power of data. Data is the canvas on which you paint the portrait of your problem, revealing patterns, trends, and insights that might otherwise remain hidden.

1: Collecting Relevant Data

Effective data analysis begins with collecting the right data. In our age of information overload, it's crucial to focus on data that directly relates to the problem at hand. This could include customer feedback, production records, financial statements, or any other information pertinent to your specific issue.

2: Visualizing Your Data

Numbers and statistics can be overwhelming, but visualizations like charts, graphs, and histograms can transform raw data into actionable insights. Visual representations make it easier to spot trends, anomalies, and areas of focus. Tools like Pareto charts, which prioritize issues based on frequency or impact, are particularly useful in this context.

3: The Art of Pattern Recognition

As you delve into your data, keep an open mind and let patterns emerge. Look for recurring themes, correlations, and outliers. These insights can lead to a deeper understanding of the problem's nuances and potential solutions.

Implementing Effective Solutions

With a clear understanding of the core issues and data-driven insights in hand, it's time to roll up your sleeves and implement effective solutions. This is where the rubber meets the road, where your problem-solving skills come to life, and where positive change begins to take shape.

1: Setting SMART Goals

Before you take action, it's essential to define your goals with precision. The SMART criteria—Specific, Measurable, Achievable, Relevant, and Time-bound—provide a framework for creating clear and actionable objectives.

For example, if your core issue is high employee turnover, a SMART goal might be, "Reduce employee turnover by 20% within the next six months by implementing a mentorship program and conducting regular feedback sessions."

2: Experimentation and Continuous Improvement

Not all solutions will work perfectly on the first try, and that's okay. Pareto-driven problem-solving encourages experimentation and a willingness to adapt. Implement your solution, measure its impact, and be ready to make adjustments based on the data.

3: The Power of Feedback Loops

Feedback loops are invaluable in the implementation phase. They allow you to gather input from stakeholders, employees, or customers to fine-tune your solutions continually. Whether through surveys, focus groups, or regular check-ins, feedback keeps your solutions aligned with the evolving needs of your problem-solving journey.

Pareto-driven problem-solving is a potent approach that empowers you to navigate life's challenges with precision and efficiency. By identifying core issues, leveraging data analysis, and implementing effective solutions, you unlock the potential to turn obstacles into opportunities. This journey is not only about problem-solving but also about personal growth, resilience, and the pursuit of excellence. As you apply these principles in your life, you'll discover that the path to success is clearer and more achievable than ever before.

12.2 Decision Making for Success

In this sub-chapter, we're going to delve deep into the art of decision making and explore how the Pareto principle can be your trusty compass in navigating the treacherous waters of choices. Decisions, big or small, have a profound impact on our lives. They can either propel us toward our goals or leave us feeling lost in a sea of uncertainty. By applying the Pareto principle to your decision-making process, you can not only make better choices but also unlock the door to a more successful and fulfilling life.

Rational Decision Making with Pareto

Picture this: You're at a crossroads, faced with a major life decision. It could be about a career change, a relationship, or a financial investment. You're grappling with the weight of the decision, unsure of which path to take. This is where rational decision making, guided by the Pareto principle, comes into play.

Rational decision making begins with a crystal-clear understanding of your goals and values. What are your core priorities in life? What do you truly value? By identifying these, you create a framework against which you can assess potential choices. Pareto's 80/20 principle reminds us that a minority of choices often yields the majority of results. In decision making, this means that a few key factors are likely to have a disproportionately significant impact on the outcome.

Start by listing the options available to you and the potential outcomes of each. Then, consider which options align most closely with your goals and values. Pareto suggests that focusing on the vital few factors that matter most can lead to more efficient and effective decisions. For example, when evaluating a job offer, consider factors like job satisfaction, growth opportunities, and work-life balance. These might outweigh a slightly higher salary if they align with your values.

Additionally, rational decision making involves gathering relevant information. Research, seek advice from experts, and assess the risks and benefits of each option. Pareto's principle encourages us to focus on the 20% of information that will likely determine 80% of the decision's outcome. This means honing in on the most critical details and filtering out the noise.

Finally, make your decision based on the insights gained from your analysis. Trust your intuition, but let it be guided by the rational framework you've established. Pareto teaches us that focusing on the key factors will not only lead to better decisions but also save us from decision fatigue and analysis paralysis. This way, you can confidently step onto the path that aligns most closely with your goals and values.

Risk Assessment and Mitigation

Every decision, no matter how well-informed, carries an element of risk. The Pareto principle can be an invaluable tool for assessing and mitigating these risks, allowing you to navigate uncertainty with greater confidence.

Start by identifying the potential risks associated with each decision you're considering. This might involve financial risks, such as investment losses, or personal risks, such as the impact on your relationships. Pareto encourages us to focus on the vital few risks that are most likely to have a significant impact on the outcome.

Next, assess the severity and probability of each risk. Pareto's 80/20 principle reminds us that a minority of risks often accounts for the majority of potential harm. Prioritize your efforts on mitigating these high-impact risks. For example, if you're launching a new business venture, focus on the critical risks that could lead to business failure, such as market competition or financial stability, rather than less impactful risks like minor operational hiccups.

Mitigating risks might involve developing contingency plans, seeking insurance, or diversifying your investments. By concentrating your resources on the vital few risks, you can proactively address potential challenges and increase your chances of success.

Remember, too, that Pareto's principle teaches us that not all risks are created equal. Some risks might be worth taking if the potential rewards align with your goals. By applying Pareto's wisdom to risk assessment, you can make informed decisions that balance the pursuit of opportunity with the mitigation of potential harm.

Strategic Decision Making

Strategic decision making is about seeing the bigger picture and understanding how your choices fit into your long-term goals. The Pareto principle can guide you in crafting a strategic approach to decision making that leads to lasting success.

Start by setting clear, well-defined goals. What are you striving to achieve in the long run? Your goals act as a compass, helping you determine whether a decision aligns with your overarching vision. Pareto's principle reminds us that a minority of our efforts often generates the majority of our results. Therefore, it's essential to focus on those decisions that move the needle toward our most significant objectives.

Consider the impact of your decisions not just in the immediate future but over time. Pareto encourages us to prioritize the factors that have the most significant long-term consequences. When making strategic decisions, think about how they will ripple through your life, affecting your career, relationships, and personal growth.

Strategic decision making also involves recognizing opportunities for synergy. Pareto's principle highlights that certain choices can have a cascading effect, positively impacting multiple areas of your life. For example, a decision to pursue a new skill or hobby might not only enhance your personal life but also open doors in your career or expand your social network.

Lastly, revisit and reassess your decisions regularly. Pareto's principle teaches us that circumstances change, and what was once a high-impact decision might need adjustment as time goes on. Be flexible and willing to adapt your choices as needed to stay aligned with your long-term goals and values.

Decision making is an art, and the Pareto principle can be your trusted paintbrush. By approaching decisions rationally, assessing and mitigating risks, and adopting a strategic mindset, you can make choices that lead to success and fulfillment. Remember, your life is a canvas, and each decision you make adds color to the masterpiece you're creating. So, choose wisely, and let the wisdom of Pareto guide you toward a future filled with purpose, prosperity, and happiness.

12.3 Ethical Considerations

In the intricate web of life, ethical dilemmas are the threads that often challenge us to make decisions with moral consequences. As we navigate our journey through the lens of Pareto efficiency, it's crucial to pause and reflect on the ethical implications of our choices. This sub-chapter delves deep into the intersection of ethics and efficiency, guiding you on how to make ethical choices while applying Pareto principles.

Ethical Dilemmas and Pareto

Ethical dilemmas are those moments when we find ourselves at a crossroads, torn between different courses of action, each carrying ethical implications. The Pareto principle, with its emphasis on optimizing resources, may seem at odds with ethical considerations. After all, how can we prioritize efficiency without sacrificing our moral compass?

The key to reconciling Pareto efficiency with ethical dilemmas lies in recognizing that ethical principles can be applied within the framework of Pareto. In fact, the 80/20 rule can be a powerful tool for identifying ethical priorities.

Consider a scenario where you're managing a team and need to decide on layoffs to improve the company's financial health. Applying Pareto, you might analyze which employees contribute the most to the organization's success. But ethical concerns arise – is it ethical to lay off employees who may be struggling due to personal circumstances?

Here, Pareto can help you make ethical choices by considering the broader impact. Prioritize employees who have alternative job opportunities or those who may benefit from a fresh start elsewhere. Focus on providing support to the employees affected by the layoffs, demonstrating that ethical considerations can coexist with efficiency.

The Balance Between Ethics and Efficiency

Striking the right balance between ethics and efficiency is an art. It's about finding that sweet spot where you optimize resources while staying true to your moral principles. To achieve this balance, start by:

1. Defining Your Ethical Framework: Clearly articulate your ethical principles and values. This foundation will serve as your compass when navigating dilemmas.

2. Identifying Ethical Red Flags: Use Pareto analysis to identify areas where ethical concerns may arise. Ask yourself: Are there potential negative consequences for a particular group or stakeholder?

3. Seeking Input: Consult with colleagues, mentors, or trusted advisors. They can provide valuable perspectives and help you consider ethical nuances.

4. Transparency: Be transparent in your decision-making process. Explain your rationale, emphasizing that you've considered ethical implications.

5. Monitoring and Adaptation: Continually evaluate the ethical impact of your decisions. Be prepared to adjust your course if unintended ethical consequences emerge.

Remember, the Pareto principle can guide you in achieving greater efficiency while still upholding ethical standards. It's not about compromising your values; it's about finding innovative ways to align them with your goals.

Making Ethical Choices

Ethical choices aren't always clear-cut, and making them can be challenging. However, Pareto can be a valuable tool in making these choices more manageable. Here's a step-by-step process to help you navigate ethical dilemmas:

1. Gather Information: Begin by collecting all relevant data and facts. Understand the potential consequences of your decisions on various stakeholders.

2. Apply Pareto Analysis: Identify the vital few factors or actions that will have the most significant ethical impact. Focus on these areas.

3. Consider Alternatives: Explore alternative courses of action that prioritize ethical considerations while still achieving your desired outcomes.

4. Consult Others: Seek input from colleagues, mentors, or ethics experts. Their perspectives can offer valuable insights and help you see blind spots.

5. Ethical Prioritization: Use Pareto to prioritize ethical principles. Determine which principles are most critical in this specific context.

6. Reflect on Long-Term Consequences: Consider the long-term ethical consequences of your decision. How will it affect your reputation, relationships, and values over time?

7. Make the Decision: Based on your analysis, make a well-informed decision that aligns with your ethical principles and goals.

8. Communication: Communicate your decision clearly and honestly, both internally and externally, if necessary.

9. Monitor and Adapt: Continually assess the ethical impact of your decision and be prepared to adjust if needed. Ethical considerations evolve, and your decisions should, too.

10. Reflect and Learn: After the decision, take time to reflect on what you've learned. Use this experience to refine your ethical decision-making process in the future.

Remember, making ethical choices within the context of Pareto principles is not about making sacrifices. Instead, it's about finding creative and efficient ways to prioritize what matters most ethically.

Ethical dilemmas need not be a roadblock on your path to Pareto-driven success. By acknowledging the ethical implications of your choices, finding the balance between ethics and efficiency, and employing a structured approach to ethical decision-making, you can navigate these challenges with integrity and purpose. In doing so, you'll not only optimize your resources but also build a reputation as a leader who upholds the highest ethical standards while achieving outstanding results.

Chapter 13: Finding Balance: Pareto for a Fulfilling Life

13.1 Personal Growth with Pareto

In this subchapter, we'll embark on an exciting journey towards personal growth and self-improvement using the power of the Pareto principle. Imagine sculpting yourself into the best version you can be, achieving your goals efficiently, and experiencing the profound joy of progress. Buckle up because we're about to dive deep into the world of personal development Pareto-style.

Setting Personal Development Goals

Have you ever felt like you're wandering aimlessly through life, unsure of where you're headed? Setting personal development goals is like setting the coordinates on your life's GPS. It provides direction, purpose, and a clear path to follow.

Pareto teaches us to identify the vital few from the trivial many. When applied to personal growth, it urges you to pinpoint the most impactful areas for improvement in your life. Instead of trying to change everything at once, focus on the 20% of actions that will yield 80% of your desired results. Pareto takes goal setting to a whole new level.

1: Identifying Your Core Goals

Pareto urges us to identify the 20% of goals that will yield 80% of our personal development results. Start by reflecting on your values and aspirations. What truly matters to you? What do you want to achieve in your life? Write these down, and then prioritize them. The Pareto principle will help you focus on the goals that will bring the most significant positive changes to your life.

2: SMART Goals and Pareto

You've likely heard of SMART goals: Specific, Measurable, Achievable, Relevant, and Time-bound. Well, Pareto and SMART goals are a match made in heaven. Apply the SMART criteria to your prioritized goals. Break them down into actionable steps and set clear deadlines. By doing this, you're not only aligning your objectives with your values, but you're also ensuring that your efforts are efficient and effective.

3: Pareto's 80/20 Goal Hacking

Now comes the Pareto magic! Once you've set your SMART goals, ask yourself, "Which 20% of these goals will bring me 80% of the personal growth I desire?" Pareto challenges you to identify the vital few goals that will have the most significant impact. It's about ruthlessly focusing your energy on what truly matters, avoiding the distractions of less important objectives.

Tracking Progress Efficiently

Setting goals is just the beginning; tracking your progress is where the magic happens. Imagine having a dashboard that shows you precisely how close you are to your personal development goals at any given time. Pareto offers you just that.

1: Pareto Progress Metrics

To apply Pareto to tracking progress, you must first identify the critical metrics related to your goals. What are the key indicators of success? If, for example, your goal is to become a more effective communicator, your metrics might include the number of presentations you've given, the number of positive feedback received, or the reduction in misunderstandings during conversations.

2: The 80/20 Progress Check-In

Regularly assess your progress against these metrics but focus on the 20% of actions that are contributing to 80% of your results. It's easy to get caught up in the minutiae of personal development, but Pareto reminds us to concentrate our efforts on the most impactful activities. Identify the actions that are driving the most progress and double down on them.

3: Adjusting Course with Pareto Insights

Pareto is not just about working hard; it's about working smart. If you find that certain actions aren't moving the needle toward your goals, be willing to pivot. Pareto teaches us to adapt and adjust our strategies as needed. Don't be afraid to let go of what's not working and invest more in what's bringing the best results.

Becoming the Best Version of Yourself

Now that you've set your goals and are diligently tracking your progress, it's time to focus on what it means to become the best version of yourself. It's not merely about achieving external success; it's about nurturing your inner growth and authenticity.

1: Embracing Continuous Learning

Pareto encourages a lifelong commitment to learning. To become your best self, you must remain curious and open to new experiences. Whether it's reading books, taking courses, or seeking mentorship, embrace opportunities for growth and development. The 20% of knowledge you acquire will lead to 80% of your personal growth.

2: Building Resilience

Personal development is not without its challenges. Life will throw curveballs, and setbacks are inevitable. However, Pareto teaches us that a small percentage of our efforts can help us build the resilience needed to bounce back from adversity. By cultivating a growth mindset, practicing self-compassion, and seeking support when needed, you'll enhance your ability to weather life's storms.

3: Balancing Success and Well-being

Pareto's wisdom extends beyond material success. It reminds us that the pursuit of happiness and well-being is equally essential. Balance your personal development journey with self-care, mindfulness, and nurturing your mental and emotional health. After all, becoming the best version of yourself isn't just about achieving goals; it's about living a fulfilling and joyful life.

As you embark on your personal development journey with Pareto as your guiding light, remember that it's not about striving for an elusive perfection. It's about efficiently channeling your efforts toward meaningful goals, embracing continuous growth, and becoming the best version of yourself—one step at a time. The Pareto principle empowers you to do just that, guiding you toward a life of purpose, fulfillment, and endless possibility.

13.2 Balancing Multiple Life Goals

Balancing Multiple Life Goals may seem like a daunting task in today's fast-paced world, but it's a crucial component of creating a fulfilling and meaningful life. In this sub-chapter, we'll explore the Pareto Approach to Multitasking, the art of Juggling Career, Family, and Hobbies, and how to Thrive in a Multifaceted Life.

The Pareto Approach to Multitasking

Let's face it: we all have busy lives. We're pulled in multiple directions - work, family, personal goals, and hobbies - and it often feels like an endless juggling act. But what if I told you that you can apply the Pareto principle to multitasking and make it work for you?

The Pareto principle, also known as the 80/20 rule, teaches us that roughly 80% of our results come from 20% of our efforts. This principle can be applied to multitasking by identifying the tasks that yield the most significant results and prioritizing them.

Here's how you can apply the Pareto Approach to Multitasking:

1: Prioritize Your Tasks

Start by making a list of all the tasks you need to juggle in your life. Then, identify the 20% of tasks that will bring you the most significant results or satisfaction. These are your high-priority tasks.

2: Time Blocking

Once you've identified your high-priority tasks, allocate specific time blocks in your schedule to focus on them. This allows you to dedicate your full attention and energy to these essential activities.

3: Batch Similar Tasks

Group similar tasks together and tackle them in one go. For example, if you have work-related emails to respond to, family commitments, and personal projects, try to batch these activities during dedicated time slots. This minimizes the mental switching cost associated with multitasking.

By applying the Pareto principle to multitasking, you can ensure that you're spending your time and energy on the most important activities in your life. It's not about doing more; it's about doing the right things efficiently.

Juggling Career, Family, and Hobbies

Balancing your career, family, and personal interests can be challenging, but it's also incredibly rewarding. Here's how you can navigate this intricate juggling act:

1: Prioritize Your Values

First and foremost, identify your core values. What truly matters to you? Is it your family, your career, or your hobbies? Understanding your values will help you make decisions that align with your priorities.

2: Effective Time Management

Time management is the key to successfully juggling these aspects of your life. Use techniques like time blocking and setting boundaries to allocate time to each area without feeling overwhelmed.

3: Delegate and Seek Support

Don't be afraid to delegate tasks when possible. Whether it's at work or at home, seeking support from others can alleviate some of the burdens and create more balance in your life.

Thrive in a Multifaceted Life

Thriving in a multifaceted life isn't just about managing your time; it's also about nurturing your well-being and finding joy in the journey. Here's how you can thrive in the midst of it all:

1: Embrace Flexibility

Life is unpredictable, and sometimes, you'll need to adapt to unexpected changes. Embrace flexibility and learn to go with the flow when necessary.

2: Self-Care Is Non-Negotiable

Amidst all the responsibilities, don't forget to take care of yourself. Prioritize self-care and make time for activities that recharge your physical and mental well-being.

3: Celebrate Small Wins

In a multifaceted life, it's easy to get caught up in the hustle and bustle. Take a moment to celebrate your small victories, whether it's a successful work project, quality time with family, or progress in your hobbies.

Remember, a fulfilling life is not about achieving a perfect balance every day; it's about finding harmony over time. Your career, family, and hobbies can coexist and enrich each other. It's in the ebb and flow of these elements that you'll discover the true essence of a multifaceted, meaningful life.

As you navigate the intricate dance of balancing multiple life goals, keep in mind that it's not about perfection but about finding joy and fulfillment in the journey. Embrace the Pareto Approach to Multitasking, prioritize your values, and nurture your well-being. In doing so, you'll find that the juggling act becomes less daunting, and you can truly thrive in a multifaceted life.

13.3 Pursuing Passion Projects

In our fast-paced, goal-oriented lives, it's easy to get caught up in the pursuit of success and forget about the activities that truly light up our souls. These are the hobbies and passion projects that bring us joy, fuel our creativity, and provide a sense of fulfillment beyond measure. In this sub-chapter, we'll explore how you can apply Pareto principles to make room for your passion pursuits, effectively manage your time, and even turn these passions into side hustles that can enhance your life in more ways than one.

Pareto-Driven Passion Pursuits

Let's begin by acknowledging that pursuing your passion projects isn't a frivolous indulgence but a vital aspect of leading a fulfilling life. These activities serve as an oasis of creativity and joy in the desert of routine responsibilities.

The Pareto principle applies here in a profound way. Imagine that 20% of your passions bring you 80% of your happiness and creative fulfillment. It's time to identify those core activities that truly ignite your spirit.

1. Identifying Your Core Passions: Start by reflecting on what activities bring you the most joy and satisfaction. Is it painting, writing, playing a musical instrument, gardening, or something entirely different? Make a list of these core passions.

2. Prioritizing Your Time: Now, take a closer look at your schedule. Are you dedicating time to these core passions regularly, or have they been pushed aside by the demands

of daily life? The Pareto principle encourages us to prioritize the 20% that matters most.

3. Eliminating the Non-Essential: Often, we find ourselves engaged in activities that don't align with our passions but consume a significant amount of our time. Identify these time-wasters and consider cutting back on them to create space for what truly matters.

4. Setting Specific Goals: Just as in other areas of life, setting clear and achievable goals for your passion projects is essential. What do you want to accomplish? It could be completing a novel, holding an art exhibition, or mastering a musical piece. Pareto reminds us to focus on the vital few goals that will make the most significant impact on your creative journey.

5. Consistency is Key: Once you've identified your core passions and set specific goals, the key is to remain consistent in your efforts. Pareto's principle encourages us to put our energy into the activities that yield the most significant results, and for passion projects, consistency is often the key to success.

Remember, the goal here is not just to pursue your passions occasionally but to make them an integral part of your daily or weekly routine. By applying the Pareto principle, you can channel your energy into the activities that truly matter and experience a deeper sense of fulfillment.

Managing Time for Hobbies

One common challenge many of us face when it comes to pursuing our passion projects is finding the time. Our busy lives can make it seem almost impossible to carve out space for hobbies and creative endeavors. However, with Pareto's wisdom, we can unlock the secret to time management that supports our passions.

1. Time Tracking: Start by tracking how you spend your time each day. This can be an eye-opening exercise, as it will reveal where your time is going. Are you spending hours on tasks that bring little joy or value to your life? Pareto encourages us to eliminate or delegate these low-value activities.

2. Time Blocking: One effective time management technique that aligns with the Pareto principle is time blocking. Allocate specific blocks of time in your schedule for your passion projects. This dedicated time allows you to immerse yourself fully in your creative pursuits.

3. Prioritization: As we've discussed earlier, identifying the 20% of your activities that contribute to 80% of your happiness is crucial. Make these passion projects a priority in your schedule. By focusing on the vital few, you'll naturally reduce the time spent on less fulfilling activities.

4. Setting Boundaries: In our hyper-connected world, it's easy for work and other commitments to spill over into our personal time. Set clear boundaries to protect your passion project time. Let others know when you're unavailable and prioritize your creative moments.

5. Time Efficiency Techniques: Pareto's principle encourages us to find ways to achieve more with less effort. Apply this mindset to your creative pursuits by exploring time-efficient techniques. For example, if you're a writer, learn to write more in less time without compromising quality.

6. Delegate or Outsource: If certain tasks are eating up a significant portion of your time and can be delegated or outsourced, consider doing so. This allows you to reclaim precious hours for your passion projects.

7. Practice Self-Care: Remember that self-care is not a luxury but a necessity. Maintaining your physical and mental well-being ensures you have the energy and focus to pursue your passions effectively.

By strategically managing your time using Pareto's principles, you'll discover that finding time for your passion projects becomes not only possible but also deeply rewarding.

Turning Passions into Side Hustles

What if you could not only enjoy your passion projects but also turn them into a source of income? The Pareto approach encourages us to explore the opportunities that can arise from our core passions.

1. Identifying Marketable Skills: Start by recognizing the skills you've developed through your passion projects. These skills, whether in art, writing, music, or any other field, can be valuable in the marketplace.

2. Market Research: Investigate the demand for your passion-related skills or products. Is there a market for what you create or offer? Pareto's principle reminds us to focus on the areas where our efforts will yield the most significant returns.

3. Building Your Brand: In the digital age, it's easier than ever to showcase your work and build a personal brand around your passions. Social media, personal websites, and online communities can help you connect with potential clients or customers.

4. Monetization Strategies: Explore different monetization strategies that align with your passion projects. This might include selling artwork, publishing books, offering online courses, or providing freelance services related to your expertise.

5. Balancing Passion and Profit: While it's exciting to turn your passions into side hustles, it's essential to maintain a balance between your creative fulfillment and financial goals. Remember that your passion projects should always bring you joy and satisfaction, even as you earn from them.

6. Continuous Learning: Just as in any business venture, ongoing learning and adaptation are key. Stay open to new opportunities and be willing to pivot if necessary.

By applying Pareto's principles to your passion projects, you can not only find time to pursue what you love but also explore the potential for financial rewards. It's a powerful way to create a fulfilling and sustainable lifestyle that combines creativity with financial independence.

Your passion projects are not just hobbies; they're pathways to a more fulfilling and balanced life. Remember, the vital few activities that truly matter should always take precedence, and your passions are undeniably among them. So, go ahead, embrace your creative side, and let the Pareto principle guide.

Chapter 14: Managing Stress and Burnout with Pareto

14.1 Stress Reduction Strategies

In our fast-paced, modern lives, stress has become an all-too-familiar companion. It seems as though the demands of daily life keep increasing, and stress, unfortunately, is an unwelcome side effect. But what if I told you that the Pareto principle, the very one that has guided us through this remarkable journey, can be harnessed to not only identify stressors but also mitigate their impact? Stress reduction is not just about eliminating all stressors but strategically addressing the ones that matter most. So, let's delve into the art of stress reduction with Pareto.

Identifying Stress Triggers

The first step on our journey to conquer stress is to recognize its sources. Stressors come in various shapes and sizes, and they often lurk beneath the surface, causing havoc in our lives without us even realizing it. By applying the Pareto principle, we can discern the vital few stressors from the trivial many.

Life's stressors can be grouped into two categories: the vital few and the trivial many. The vital few are those that have the most significant impact on our well-being and should be our primary focus for mitigation. Identifying these stress triggers requires introspection and self-awareness. Here's how you can start:

- Stress Journaling: Keeping a stress journal can be a powerful tool. Each day, jot down the events or situations that made you feel stressed. Over time, patterns will emerge, revealing the recurring sources of stress in your life.

- Physical and Emotional Signals: Pay attention to your body and emotions. Are there specific physical sensations or emotional responses that consistently accompany stress? These can be valuable clues to identify your stress triggers.

- Feedback from Others: Sometimes, those close to us can see our stress triggers more clearly than we can. Don't hesitate to seek feedback from friends, family, or colleagues who may have noticed patterns in your stress responses.

Once you've identified your vital few stress triggers, you're well on your way to taking control of your stress levels. Remember, it's not about eliminating all stress but strategically addressing the ones that matter most.

Pareto Solutions for Stress
With your stress triggers identified, it's time to apply Pareto's 80/20 principle to find efficient solutions. The goal here is not to eliminate all stress but to allocate your resources, time, and energy to those solutions that will yield the most significant stress reduction.

- Prioritizing Stress Reduction: Start by identifying the vital few stressors that contribute most to your overall stress levels. These might be work-related deadlines, family conflicts, or health concerns. Focus on addressing these stressors first.

- Stressor Mitigation Strategies: For each vital stress trigger, develop a tailored mitigation strategy. Consider whether you can delegate tasks, set boundaries, or seek external support to reduce the impact of these stressors.

- Stress-Reducing Habits: Incorporate stress-reducing habits into your daily routine. These can include regular exercise, mindfulness meditation, or relaxation techniques. Allocate a portion of your time to these habits, ensuring you prioritize self-care.

- The 80/20 of Relaxation: Remember that not all relaxation techniques are created equal. Pareto suggests that a small percentage of your relaxation efforts will yield most of the benefits. Experiment with different relaxation practices, and identify those that offer the most significant stress relief for you.

By applying the Pareto principle to your stress reduction efforts, you're making strategic choices that will have the most substantial impact on your overall well-being. It's about working smarter, not harder, to regain control over your life.

Relaxation and Mindfulness Techniques
Now that we've identified stress triggers and applied Pareto's efficiency principles to mitigate them, it's time to explore relaxation and mindfulness techniques that can bring peace and balance back into your life.

- Mindfulness Meditation: Mindfulness meditation is a powerful tool to manage stress. Dedicate a few minutes each day to sit quietly, focus on your breath, and observe your thoughts without judgment. This practice enhances your ability to stay present and respond to stressors calmly.

- Progressive Muscle Relaxation: This technique involves systematically tensing and then relaxing different muscle groups in your body. By doing so, you release physical tension, which can help alleviate the effects of stress.

- Deep Breathing: Simple yet effective, deep breathing exercises can be practiced anywhere. Inhale deeply through your nose, hold for a few seconds, and then exhale slowly through your mouth. This practice triggers the body's relaxation response.

- Visualization: Guided visualization exercises can transport your mind to a peaceful, stress-free place. Picture yourself in a serene environment, focusing on sensory details to immerse yourself fully in the experience.

- Yoga and Tai Chi: These practices combine physical movement, deep breathing, and mindfulness, making them excellent tools for reducing stress. Regular participation in yoga or Tai Chi classes can help you maintain a calm and centered state of mind.

- Digital Detox: Our constant connection to screens can contribute to stress. Allocate specific times during the day for digital detox, where you disconnect from screens and engage in analog activities like reading, nature walks, or hobbies.

- Gratitude Journaling: Ending your day by jotting down things you're grateful for can shift your focus from stressors to positive aspects of your life. This practice promotes a more optimistic mindset.

Remember that incorporating these relaxation and mindfulness techniques into your daily routine doesn't have to be time-consuming. By applying the Pareto principle to self-care, you can identify the most effective techniques that yield the greatest stress reduction for you. In doing so, you'll regain a sense of calm and resilience in the face of life's challenges.

14.2 Burnout Prevention and Recovery

Burnout is a relentless foe that lurks in the shadows, waiting for an opportunity to strike. It's a formidable adversary that can creep into your life when you least expect it, draining your energy, sapping your motivation, and clouding your perspective. But fear not, for Pareto is here to help you not only recognize the signs of burnout but also provide you with effective strategies for prevention and recovery.

Recognizing Burnout Signs

Before we dive into the intricacies of combating burnout with Pareto, it's crucial to recognize the warning signs.

Burnout often begins subtly, like a gentle whisper in the wind, but if left unaddressed, it can grow into a deafening storm. Here are some common indicators:

- Physical and Emotional Exhaustion: Feeling drained, physically and emotionally, even after a good night's sleep. You may find yourself perpetually tired, no matter how much rest you get.

- Cynicism and Detachment: A growing sense of cynicism and detachment from your work or personal life. You might become disengaged, pessimistic, and resentful.

- Reduced Performance: A noticeable decline in your work or personal performance. Tasks that were once routine become arduous, and your productivity takes a nosedive.

- Mental Fog: Difficulty concentrating and a persistent feeling of mental fog. Your mind might feel cluttered, making it challenging to make decisions or solve problems.

- Health Issues: Physical symptoms like headaches, stomachaches, or even more severe health problems can manifest when burnout takes its toll.

- Neglected Self-Care: Neglecting self-care activities such as exercise, proper nutrition, and spending time with loved ones.

Recognizing these signs early on is paramount to effectively combating burnout. When you acknowledge that something isn't right, you empower yourself to take action.

Pareto for Work-Life Burnout

Now that you've identified the warning signs, let's explore how Pareto can be your ally in preventing burnout, especially in the context of your work-life balance.

Key Point 1: Pareto-Driven Prioritization

Pareto reminds us that not all tasks are created equal. To prevent burnout, you must prioritize tasks based on their significance and potential impact. Identify the 20% of tasks that contribute to 80% of your stress and focus your efforts there.

Start by creating a list of your daily or weekly tasks and categorize them into high-priority and low-priority activities. High-priority tasks are those that directly contribute to your long-term goals and well-being, while low-priority tasks are often minor or can be delegated to others.

Once you've categorized your tasks, commit to tackling the high-priority ones first. This not only ensures that you're addressing the most critical aspects of your work but also helps create a sense of accomplishment and reduces the feeling of overwhelm.

Key Point 2: Setting Boundaries

One of the leading causes of burnout is overextending oneself. Learning to say "no" and setting clear boundaries is an essential part of preventing burnout. Pareto can help you here by focusing on the 20% of activities that truly matter and letting go of the less important ones.

Evaluate your commitments and responsibilities, both at work and in your personal life. Are there tasks or obligations that drain your energy without providing meaningful returns? If so, consider reallocating your time and effort towards activities that align with your goals and values.

Effective boundary-setting also involves time management. Pareto encourages you to allocate your time wisely. Use techniques like time blocking to dedicate specific periods to high-priority tasks while safeguarding time for rest, relaxation, and rejuvenation.

Key Point 3: Seeking Support and Delegation

You don't have to navigate the challenges of work and life on your own. Pareto suggests that you focus on your strengths and delegate tasks that others can handle more efficiently. By doing so, you not only free up your time but also reduce the risk of burnout.

Identify tasks that fall outside your core competencies or that others on your team could handle more effectively. Delegating responsibilities not only lightens your workload but also empowers others to contribute their skills and expertise.

Additionally, seek support from your colleagues, friends, or a mentor. Discussing your feelings of burnout with trusted individuals can provide valuable insights and emotional support. Remember, it's not a sign of weakness to ask for help—it's a sign of strength and self-awareness.

Reclaiming Your Energy and Motivation
Burnout can be a tenacious adversary, but with Pareto as your guide, you can recover and rejuvenate.

Key Point 1: Pareto-Driven Recovery Plan

Pareto principles can be instrumental in crafting an effective recovery plan. Begin by identifying the activities or habits that have contributed to your burnout. These could be overworking, neglecting self-care, or allowing stress to accumulate.

Next, prioritize your recovery efforts. Focus on the 20% of actions that will yield 80% of the results in terms of reclaiming your energy and motivation. This might involve making time for activities that bring you joy and relaxation, like exercise, meditation, or spending time with loved ones.

Key Point 2: Restoring Balance

Burnout often stems from an imbalance in your life. Pareto encourages you to evaluate how you allocate your time and resources to various aspects of your life.

Consider the various roles you play—professional, personal, and perhaps even as a caregiver or community member. Are you devoting enough time and energy to each role to maintain balance? Pareto suggests reallocating resources as needed to ensure that no single area dominates your life to the detriment of others.

Key Point 3: Goal-Setting for Renewed Purpose

As you recover from burnout, setting goals can provide a renewed sense of purpose and motivation. Pareto emphasizes that not all goals are equally important. Identify the 20% of goals that will have the most significant impact on your well-being and focus on those.

Start with small, achievable goals to build momentum. Celebrate your progress along the way, and don't forget to acknowledge your achievements, no matter how minor they may seem. Gradually, as you regain your energy and motivation, you can set more ambitious goals aligned with your long-term vision.

Combating burnout with Pareto is not only about recognizing the signs and addressing them but also about making deliberate choices in how you allocate your time and effort. By prioritizing tasks, setting boundaries, seeking support, and focusing on recovery, you can not only prevent burnout but also embark on a journey of renewed energy, motivation, and fulfillment. Remember, you have the power to reclaim your life and thrive.

14.3 Building Resilience

In the relentless whirlwind of life, stress and burnout often lurk around the corner, waiting to ambush our well-being. However, armed with the Pareto principle and a desire for a resilient spirit, you can navigate these challenges with grace, strength, and unwavering determination. In this section, we'll delve deep into the art of building resilience, both mentally and physically, to face life's tribulations with ease.

Strengthening Mental Resilience

Mental resilience is the secret weapon that empowers us to bounce back from adversity, no matter how daunting it may seem. It's the ability to weather the storm and emerge stronger on the other side. Here's how Pareto can help you fortify your mental resilience:

Key Point 1: Embrace a Growth Mindset

The foundation of mental resilience is a growth mindset. Embrace the idea that setbacks and failures are not the end but stepping stones to success. According to Pareto, 80% of your progress comes from the 20% of efforts you invest in learning and adapting. When you view challenges as opportunities for growth, you unlock your inner potential.

Key Point 2: Strategic Problem Solving

Pareto suggests that 20% of problems often cause 80% of your stress. Instead of getting overwhelmed by the sheer volume of issues, focus on identifying and addressing the core problems. This targeted approach not only conserves your mental energy but also provides effective solutions.

Key Point 3: Mindfulness and Emotional Regulation

Mindfulness, a practice rooted in the Pareto principle, can significantly enhance your mental resilience. It encourages you to be present in the moment and acknowledge your emotions without judgment. The power lies in realizing that 20% of your emotional reactions often stem from 80% of your thoughts. By practicing mindfulness, you can gain better control over your reactions and maintain emotional equilibrium during challenging times.

Physical Well-being and Resilience

A strong body forms the basis for a resilient mind. Physical well-being isn't just about exercise and diet; it's about embracing a holistic approach to health that aligns with Pareto's efficiency principles.

Key Point 1: Optimize Sleep for Recovery

Quality sleep is the unsung hero of resilience. Pareto teaches us that focusing on the critical 20% of activities can yield 80% of results. The same applies to sleep. Concentrate on improving the essential 20% of your sleep habits, such as sleep duration and consistency, to reap 80% of the benefits. A well-rested body can tackle stressors more effectively.

Key Point 2: Efficient Exercise Routine

Many people feel overwhelmed by the idea of maintaining a rigorous exercise regimen. Pareto suggests an alternative approach: focus on the 20% of exercises that deliver 80% of the results. High-intensity interval training (HIIT) and compound exercises, for instance, offer maximum benefits in minimal time. By optimizing your workouts, you can build physical resilience without dedicating hours to the gym.

Key Point 3: Nutrition for Energy and Focus

When it comes to nutrition, Pareto advocates for making smart choices that provide the most significant impact. Concentrate on the 20% of foods that offer 80% of the nutrients your body needs. A diet rich in whole grains, lean proteins, fruits, and vegetables can boost your energy levels and enhance mental clarity, making it easier to withstand the pressures of daily life.

Navigating Life's Challenges with Ease
Resilience isn't just about bouncing back; it's also about gracefully navigating life's twists and turns. Pareto's principles can guide you in finding ease amidst chaos.

Key Point 1: Effective Time Management

Pareto's 80/20 rule applies beautifully to time management. Identify the 20% of activities that yield 80% of your desired outcomes, and prioritize them. This approach helps you allocate your energy and time efficiently, reducing stress caused by time constraints.

Key Point 2: Leverage Support Systems

Pareto teaches us that collaborations and relationships contribute significantly to success. Lean on your support system during challenging times. Focus on the 20% of relationships that provide 80% of your emotional support. Share your burdens, seek advice, and offer your support in return. Together, you can navigate life's challenges more effectively.

Key Point 3: Adapt and Pivot

Resilience isn't synonymous with stubbornness. Pareto encourages flexibility and adaptability. Recognize that 20% of your actions often lead to 80% of your adaptability in times of change. By embracing change with an open mind and a willingness to adjust your course, you'll find that life's challenges become opportunities for growth rather than sources of stress.

Building resilience with Pareto's principles isn't just about surviving; it's about thriving. Strengthening your mental and physical well-being while navigating life's challenges with ease allows you to emerge from adversity not as a survivor but as a resilient conqueror. Embrace the Pareto way, and you'll discover that even in the face of stress and burnout, your inner strength can shine brighter than ever before.

Chapter 15: The Pareto Lifestyle Transformation

15.1 Embracing a New Way of Living

In this section, we delve into the profound journey of embracing a Pareto-inspired lifestyle. It's about reevaluating your priorities, letting go of what no longer serves you, and crafting a life that aligns perfectly with your goals.

Revisiting Your Priorities

In the hustle and bustle of modern life, it's all too easy to lose sight of what truly matters to us. We find ourselves caught up in the daily grind, chasing deadlines, and striving to keep up with the demands of society. It's a familiar script, one that many of us have followed for years.

But now, it's time to press pause, to revisit the script, and to rewrite it in a way that resonates deeply with your values and desires. This process begins with a simple yet profound question: What are your priorities?

Identifying your priorities is the cornerstone of living a life that aligns with the Pareto principle. It's about recognizing that not all tasks, commitments, or activities are created equal. In fact, a significant portion of our efforts often yields minimal results. By revisiting your priorities, you can pinpoint those essential few tasks that truly make a difference.

Start by taking a step back and reflecting on what brings you joy, fulfillment, and a sense of purpose. Is it spending quality time with loved ones, pursuing your passion, contributing to your community, or excelling in your career? Your priorities may encompass a combination of these and more.

Once you've identified your priorities, it becomes easier to allocate your time and energy accordingly. Pareto's 80/20 rule comes into play here—focus your efforts on the 20% of activities that yield 80% of your desired outcomes. By doing so, you're not only reclaiming precious time but also moving closer to a life that truly reflects your values.

Letting Go of What No Longer Serves You
Now that you've identified your priorities, it's time to shed the excess baggage that's been holding you back. We often accumulate commitments, possessions, and even relationships that no longer serve our goals and values. These can weigh us down and hinder our progress towards a more fulfilling life.

Imagine your life as a garden. To cultivate a beautiful and thriving garden, you must prune away the dead branches and weeds that hinder growth. Similarly, in your life, it's essential to let go of anything that no longer contributes positively to your journey.

Start by conducting a thorough assessment of your commitments, both professional and personal. Are there tasks that drain your energy and provide little value? Are there obligations that you've outgrown or that no longer align with your priorities? It may be time to delegate, renegotiate, or, in some cases, let go altogether.

The process of decluttering isn't limited to your schedule; it extends to your physical and digital spaces. Tidy up your living environment, get rid of possessions that no longer bring you joy, and declutter your digital life by organizing files and cleaning up your online presence. A clutter-free space can lead to a clutter-free mind, allowing you to focus on what truly matters.

Moreover, consider your relationships. Are there individuals who drain your energy or are toxic to your well-being? While it can be challenging, it's essential to create healthy boundaries and distance yourself from negativity. Surround yourself with people who uplift and inspire you, nurturing relationships that align with your journey towards a Pareto-inspired life.

Creating a Life Aligned with Your Goals

With your priorities clarified and excess baggage shed, it's time to craft a life that aligns seamlessly with your goals. This is where the true magic of the Pareto lifestyle transformation begins to unfold.

Start by setting clear, specific goals that reflect your priorities. Whether it's excelling in your career, achieving personal growth milestones, or making a meaningful impact in your community, your goals should be the guiding stars that illuminate your path.

Next, break these goals down into actionable steps. Pareto's principle reminds us that not all actions are created equal. Identify the critical 20% of actions that will yield 80% of your desired results. This approach ensures that your efforts are focused and efficient, allowing you to make steady progress toward your goals.

It's important to cultivate a growth mindset—a belief that your abilities and intelligence can be developed through dedication and hard work. This mindset empowers you to embrace challenges, learn from setbacks, and persist in the face of adversity. Remember that the Pareto principle doesn't guarantee instant success; it encourages consistent and deliberate effort towards your goals.

As you embark on this journey of transformation, surround yourself with inspiration and motivation. Seek out mentors, books, and communities that align with your values and aspirations. Their wisdom and support can be invaluable on your path to living a life that epitomizes the Pareto principle.

Embracing a Pareto-inspired lifestyle is about realigning your priorities, shedding what no longer serves you, and crafting a life that harmonizes with your goals and values. It's a journey of self-discovery and empowerment, where you reclaim your time and energy to invest in what truly matters. Your Pareto-transformed life is a life of purpose, fulfillment, and extraordinary efficiency—ready to make every moment count.

15.2 The Art of Simplicity

In a world often marked by excess, complexity, and an ever-accelerating pace of life, simplicity stands as a beacon of tranquility and wisdom. The art of simplicity, inspired by the Pareto principle, invites us to declutter our lives, both physically and mentally, and discover the profound freedom that comes with having less. In this sub-chapter, we'll delve into the three key aspects of the art of simplicity: streamlining your material possessions, digital decluttering and minimalism, and the liberating power of embracing less.

Streamlining Your Material Possessions

Imagine walking into your home and feeling an immediate sense of calm and serenity, knowing that everything you own serves a purpose and brings you joy. This is the essence of streamlining your material possessions—a journey towards a clutter-free and harmonious living space.

Start by taking a critical look at your belongings. What do you truly need, and what can you let go of? Apply the 80/20 rule, focusing on the items that bring you the most utility and happiness while letting go of the rest. Whether it's clothes, gadgets, or household items, pare down your possessions to the essentials.

Minimalism, an art form in itself, can be your guide. Consider the minimalist's mantra: "less is more." By embracing this philosophy, you'll not only reduce physical clutter but also create mental space for clarity and creativity.

The benefits of streamlining your material possessions extend beyond the physical realm. You'll discover that you spend less time cleaning, organizing, and managing your stuff, leaving you with more time and energy for pursuits that truly matter. As you simplify, you'll find that you're no longer burdened by the weight of excess belongings, but rather liberated to focus on what truly brings you fulfillment.

Digital Decluttering and Minimalism

In an era dominated by technology and the digital realm, our digital lives can become just as cluttered and overwhelming as our physical spaces—if not more so. Digital decluttering and minimalism are vital skills for navigating this digital age with ease and clarity.

Start by evaluating your digital habits. How many apps, emails, or files do you have that you rarely use or need? Apply the Pareto principle here by identifying the digital tools and platforms that provide the most value to you. Unsubscribe from newsletters that no longer interest you, delete redundant apps, and organize your digital files efficiently.

Embrace minimalism in your digital life by focusing on quality over quantity. Rather than having numerous apps that serve similar purposes, choose a select few that excel in their functions. Simplify your online presence by curating your social media connections and limiting your screen time. This not only reduces digital noise but also frees up mental bandwidth for more meaningful activities.

As you embark on this digital decluttering journey, you'll find that you regain a sense of control and focus in the digital world. The reduced distractions and digital simplicity will allow you to concentrate on your goals and engage more deeply with the content and connections that truly matter.

The Freedom of Less

Now, let's explore the profound sense of freedom that comes with embracing less in both your physical and digital life. Contrary to the conventional belief that more possessions and commitments lead to happiness, the art of simplicity teaches us that less can indeed be more fulfilling.

By streamlining your material possessions, you reduce the need for maintenance, organization, and storage. This translates into more time and energy for experiences and relationships that enrich your life. The freedom of less material clutter enables you to travel lightly through life, unburdened by the weight of excess baggage.

In the digital realm, embracing digital decluttering and minimalism grants you the freedom to focus on what truly matters. You'll find it easier to disconnect from the constant buzz of notifications and distractions, allowing you to be present in the moment and cultivate a deeper sense of mindfulness.

Simplicity also leads to financial freedom. As you become more mindful of your spending habits and refrain from accumulating unnecessary possessions, you'll find your savings growing. This financial freedom can provide you with opportunities to pursue your passions, invest in personal development, or even contribute to causes you care about.

Moreover, simplicity enhances your decision-making capabilities. With fewer choices to consider, you can make decisions more swiftly and with greater confidence. This efficiency extends to your daily routines, allowing you to navigate life's challenges with ease and grace.

As you embrace the art of simplicity, you'll discover a sense of liberation that permeates every aspect of your life. The freedom of less fosters a deep connection with your true values and priorities, guiding you towards a more purposeful and fulfilling existence.

The art of simplicity, influenced by the Pareto principle, is a transformative journey that empowers you to declutter your life physically and digitally, leading to the profound freedom of less. By streamlining your material possessions and embracing digital decluttering, you create space for clarity, creativity, and mindfulness. The freedom that simplicity offers extends to your finances, decision-making, and overall well-being, paving the way for a more purposeful and fulfilling life. As you embark on this journey, remember that the true essence of living lies not in the accumulation of possessions but in the pursuit of a simpler, more meaningful existence.

15.3 Mindful Consumption

In a world that constantly bombards us with advertisements, enticing us to buy more, upgrade, and indulge, it's easy to fall into the trap of mindless consumption. But what if I told you that embracing the Pareto principle in your consumption habits could lead to a more fulfilling, intentional, and even happier life? In this sub-chapter, we're going to delve deep into the concept of mindful consumption, exploring how you can apply Pareto's wisdom to your everyday spending and lifestyle choices.

Conscious Spending and Pareto

Have you ever taken a moment to reflect on your spending habits? Many of us haven't. We swipe our credit cards or click "buy now" without considering the impact of our purchases. But here's where Pareto can guide us to a more conscious way of spending.

Key Point 1: Pareto's Lens on Spending Habits

Pareto would remind us that roughly 20% of our expenses often account for 80% of our satisfaction and utility. So, the first step toward conscious spending is to identify those few key expenses that truly enhance your life. It might be that monthly yoga class, the quality coffee beans you savor every morning, or the books that expand your mind.

Key Point 2: Eliminating the Trivial Many

On the flip side, Pareto suggests that about 80% of our spending might be going towards items or services that contribute very little to our well-being. Think about those unused gym memberships, impulse purchases, or subscriptions you hardly use. By eliminating or reducing these trivial expenses, you free up resources to invest in what truly matters to you.

Key Point 3: The Joy of Value-Based Spending

By consciously allocating your resources to what brings you joy and fulfillment, you not only save money but also cultivate a sense of purpose and intentionality. Each purchase becomes a deliberate choice that aligns with your values and long-term goals.

Sustainable Choices

Mindful consumption goes beyond just spending wisely; it also extends to the impact our choices have on the planet. Sustainability has become a global concern, and the Pareto principle can guide us in making eco-conscious decisions.

Key Point 1: Pareto's Eco-Ethical Approach

Pareto's principle encourages us to recognize that a small percentage of our choices can have a significant environmental impact. By identifying these choices, such as reducing single-use plastics, conserving energy, or supporting eco-friendly brands, you can contribute to a more sustainable future.

Key Point 2: Making Small Changes for Big Impact

It's easy to feel overwhelmed by the daunting environmental challenges we face. However, Pareto's wisdom reminds us that small, consistent changes can lead to substantial results. Whether it's using reusable shopping bags, cutting down on meat consumption, or opting for public transport, your efforts can add up to significant positive change.

Key Point 3: Cultivating Eco-Gratitude

Mindful consumption isn't just about what you do; it's also about your perspective. Gratitude is a powerful tool in this journey. By appreciating the resources and products you have and their impact on your life, you'll naturally gravitate toward more sustainable choices.

Nurturing a Gratitude-Driven Lifestyle

Gratitude is the secret sauce that can transform your life. When combined with the Pareto principle, it becomes a potent force for creating a more fulfilling and content existence.

Key Point 1: Pareto's Gratitude Focus

Pareto's lens helps us recognize that a small fraction of our possessions and experiences contributes significantly to our happiness. By shifting our focus to these elements, we naturally cultivate gratitude for the abundance already present in our lives.

Key Point 2: The Ripple Effect of Gratitude

Gratitude isn't just a personal feeling; it's contagious and can positively impact your relationships and interactions with others. When you express appreciation for the people, experiences, and opportunities you've been blessed with, you create a ripple effect of positivity that can transform your connections.

Key Point 3: Gratitude as a Daily Practice

To fully embrace a gratitude-driven lifestyle, consider incorporating a daily gratitude practice into your routine. Whether it's journaling, expressing appreciation to loved ones, or simply taking a moment to savor life's small pleasures, these habits can lead to a profound shift in your overall well-being.

The Pareto principle can guide us toward a more intentional, sustainable, and fulfilling way of living. By practicing mindful consumption, making eco-conscious choices, and nurturing a gratitude-driven lifestyle, you can tap into the immense power of the 80/20 rule to create a life that truly resonates with your values and aspirations. Remember, it's not about denying yourself; it's about making choices that align with your true desires and leave you feeling content and purposeful.

Conclusion: Becoming a Pareto Master

Reflecting on Your Journey

Ah, my fellow traveler on the path of Pareto, here we stand at the threshold of transformation. It's time to pause and take a deep breath, to reflect on the profound journey you've undertaken, the journey of becoming a Pareto Master.

Reviewing Your Personal Growth

As you look back on your journey, think about the person you were when you first cracked open the pages of this book. Remember those initial doubts, the skepticism, and perhaps even the fear of change? It's all part of the process, the natural resistance we feel when embarking on a journey of self-improvement.

Now, fast forward to the present moment. Look at the incredible growth you've experienced. You've internalized the essence of the Pareto principle, the art of doing more with less. You've witnessed the magic of the 80/20 rule in action, in your career, relationships, and personal development.

Maybe you've trimmed away the excess in your life, simplifying your surroundings, and embracing a minimalist lifestyle that brings clarity and peace. Perhaps you've harnessed the power of focused effort, honing in on the vital few tasks that propel you toward your goals while discarding the trivial many.

Remember the times when you felt overwhelmed? Those moments when you thought success required endless toil and effort? You've discovered the beauty of efficiency. You've learned that it's not about how much you do but about what you do. It's about selecting the right activities that bring you the greatest results and satisfaction.

Reflect on the challenges you've faced and the obstacles you've conquered. Recall the moments when you chose the path of least resistance, the path that aligns with the Pareto way, and how it changed the game for you.

As you review your personal growth, celebrate your victories, no matter how small they may seem. Each step forward, each improvement, each moment of clarity has brought you closer to mastering the Pareto principle. It's a journey worth applauding.

Continued Application of Pareto Principles
But this journey doesn't end here. Mastery is not a destination but a lifelong pursuit. You now possess a powerful tool, the Pareto principle, that you can apply in every aspect of your life. You've witnessed its effectiveness, but the real magic lies in your continued application of these principles.

As you move forward, keep the Pareto lens on hand, ready to examine and reevaluate your choices, your actions, and your priorities. Remember that the world is in a constant state of change, and so are you. What worked yesterday may need adjustment tomorrow.

In your career, look for opportunities to focus on high-impact tasks. Seek ways to delegate or eliminate low-value activities. Continually assess your goals and strategies, making sure they align with the vital few.

In your personal life, apply Pareto principles to your relationships, your hobbies, and your well-being. Invest your time and energy in what truly matters. Let go of the clutter, both physical and mental, that holds you back.

The Pareto mindset extends to your finances, your health, your creativity, and your happiness. It's a compass that guides you toward a life of abundance, a life where you achieve more with less effort.

Embracing Lifelong Learning and Efficiency

One of the most remarkable facets of your journey as a Pareto Master is the realization that learning never ends. In fact, it's the key to sustaining your efficiency and success.

Think of yourself as a perpetual student of life, always curious, always seeking ways to improve. Stay open to new ideas, new technologies, and new approaches. Embrace change as an opportunity for growth rather than a threat.

Efficiency and the Pareto principle are not static concepts. They evolve with time, as do the challenges and opportunities you face. The more you learn, the more adept you become at applying these principles in innovative ways.

Make it a habit to seek knowledge, whether through books, courses, mentors, or experiences. Feed your mind with wisdom from diverse sources. Learn from your own experiences, both successes and failures, and be willing to adapt and refine your strategies.

Remember that becoming a Pareto Master is not about perfection but progress. It's about making incremental improvements, one step at a time. It's about choosing to be efficient, not just when it's easy, but especially when it's challenging.

As you embrace lifelong learning, you're not only enhancing your own life but also becoming an inspiration to others. You become a beacon of possibility, a living testament to the incredible transformation that's possible when one adopts the Pareto way.

So, my fellow traveler, as we conclude this remarkable journey, know that you are now equipped with the tools, the mindset, and the wisdom to navigate life's twists and turns with grace and efficiency. The world is your canvas, and the Pareto principle is your brush, allowing you to create a masterpiece of success, fulfillment, and happiness.

This is not the end; it's just the beginning. Embrace the Pareto way, and let it continue to shape your life to success and winning. Share your knowledge, inspire those around you, and leave a legacy of efficiency and excellence. Your journey as a Pareto Master has no bounds, and the adventure ahead is bound to be extraordinary.